EXISTENTIAL COMEDY
LAUGHING THROUGH THE ABSURD

Sherry Punch, PhD

Copyright © 2026 by Sherry Punch, PhD

All rights reserved. No portion of this book may be reproduced in any form without written permission from the publisher or author, except as permitted by U.S. copyright law.

Published by Existential Pantry Press

EXISTENTIAL PANTRY
FOOD FOR THOUGHT & SOUL

Website: www.existentialpantry.com

First Edition: January 2026

ISBN: 978-1-971571-00-3

Book Cover Design by Stacy D'Aguiar, www.behance.net/stacydaguiar

Illustrations generated using AI technology, Google Gemini

***Disclaimer & Limitations of Liability ***

This publication is written to entertain, provoke thought, and highlight the absurdities of life. The sale stipulates that the author and publisher offer no professional counsel, whether legal, psychological, or philosophical. While every effort has been made to present humorous and reflective content, neither the author nor the publisher makes any guarantees regarding the completeness or correctness of the ideas. The insights, observations, and existential musings in this book may not apply to your personal circumstances, and any actions you take based on them are at your own risk. Neither the author nor the publisher shall be liable for any losses, damages, or personal consequences arising from the use–or–misinterpretation of the content, including but not limited to incidental, consequential, or existential distress.

DEDICATED

To Those Who Made Me Possible

To my parents, my children, my muse, and fellow oddballs: thank you for keeping my Skelton upright, my punchlines sharp, and my absurdities tolerable. Without you, this book would be nothing more than dry bones.

Ever the punchline,

Dr. Sherry Punch :)

ACKNOWLEDGEMENTS

Every punchline needs a setup

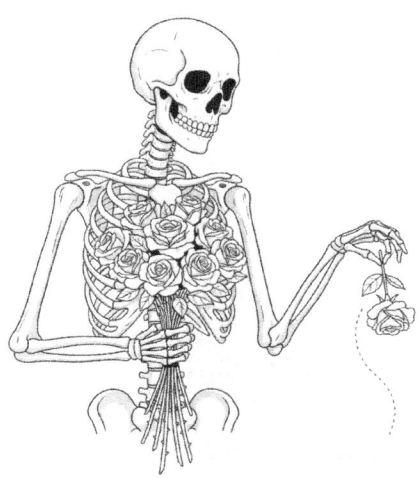

    I am indebted to my teachers, mentors, colleagues and students, who challenged me to think, question, and laugh at myself along this journey. To my writing companions and readers who braved the wildness of my drafts, my tangents, and my chaotic kitchen experiments, you're the real MVPs. Special thanks to those whose stories, humor, and pure humanity inspired these pages; your influence runs deeper than any skeletal structure. I am thankful for every bone in my body, pun intended. Finally, the everyday people and creatures around me have enriched this foundation. Without all of you, this book would be a skeleton lacking a humorous heartbeat.

BARE BONES: PREFACE

WARNING: CURIOSITY AHEAD; HANDLE WITH HUMOR.

My first existential comedy began in a funeral parlor. I was a kid, forced to stand in front of my grandmother's open casket. Though she was motionless, I was sure she was alive. Only years later did I understand my chest mirrored what I saw. That was my debut performance in the theater of life and death: a small child, a big misunderstanding, and the beginning of a lifetime of curiosity.

Fast-forward a decade. Barely two weeks out of high school, I joined the military and left my small town behind. While the Navy offered an eye-opening, sometimes light-hearted torturing adventure, I knew this was not where I wanted the years of my life to unfold. After leaving this structured discipline, I applied for a job at a funeral home. The undertaker–the supposed guardian of the afterlife–said I had to go to mortuary school. My mother, ever the comic relief, said, "Honey, I think you'd do better working with the living. You're full of light." She had a point, and for once, I actually listened.

I've always had a taste for the dark: researching serial killers, watching true crime, and studying human behavior and forensic pathology. It captivated me. I've always been curious about the stories the bones might tell if they could speak. I envision them colorless and dimmed by the sun, silently observing recollections. Perhaps a whisper of sound, a dry rattle as they shift in the earth, and the faint, metallic tang of old blood lingering in the air. Long before I earned a Ph.D. in psychology, I spent fifteen years as a professional chef, learning that I was skilled at feeding people with laughter as much as with food, tossing off one-liners like a forensic pathologist tosses surgical gloves. Following that, I earned a master's degree in forensic psychology and a Ph.D., maintaining a curious and respectful interest in corpses. While my resume pointed toward death, my life kept drifting toward kitchens, classrooms, and comedy.

Nope, I didn't become a forensic pathologist. Yet in a way, this book is my reimagined autopsy table. Each chapter is a "bone" from my story, guiding you through the Skull of Curiosity, the Rib of Regret, the Funny Bone of Folly, and more, ready for your examination. Together, they form a thematic skeleton: a body of work about life's absurdity, stitched together not with sutures, but with humor.

You don't have to read this book in order. Pick a bone, gnaw on it, or skip to the Humerus–or Humorous–at the end where the punchline waits. While you handle these bones, I hope you feel less scared of life's stillness, more amused by its movement, and even laugh while breathing.

To my mind, this book delves into subjects beyond death, humor, and psychology. The kind that separates tragedy from a punchline, a heartbreak from a breakthrough, and a funeral from a curtain call. Every loss, every absurd moment of confusion, every misplaced breath in front of an existential coffin has its own rhythm, if you dare to listen. Maybe this is what I've been doing all along: learning the comic timing of being alive. So, take a seat in the front row. Life's show is still running, and the jokes are all on us. *Welcome to Existential Comedy: Laughing Through the Absurd.*

THE SKELETON AGREEMENT

A Manifesto

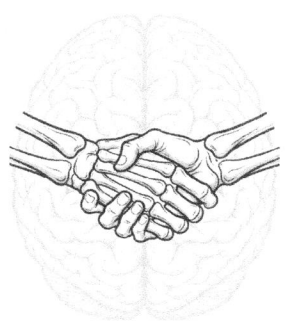

Before We Begin This Autopsy

Here is what you're signing up for: a comedic dissection of existence itself, told through the most honest framework we have: the human body. Not because bodies are complex (though they are), but because they're comically, tragically, and beautifully absurd. Our bones hold our existential struggles, our ribs carry our past regrets, and our chest harbors our worries. We are walking contradictions held together by skin and the stubborn insistence that any of this makes sense.

This book uses anatomy as a metaphor because philosophy has lingered in the clouds for too long. Existentialism belongs in the body: in the skull that won't stop generating questions at three in the morning, the heart that keeps beating despite itself, and the bones that hold us upright as we tumble through the magnificent nonsense of being alive. Thought alone cannot handle the weight of being human; it collapses under its own importance. The body, meanwhile, just shrugs and keeps breathing. The skull rolls its eyes, the heart sighs, and the bones hope someone remembers to stretch.

What This Book Is

This is existentialism with its shoes off. Rigorous enough to honor the philosophers who wrestled with meaning, yet accessible enough that you do not need a degree to get the joke. We cite Albert Camus and cry over onions while explaining to a confused child that the layers are tragic, though not as tragic as being human. We examine Sartre's idea of bad faith while finding humor in our own dishonesty, as we promise to begin the project without fail the next day. Each chapter is bone. Each bone carries a fragment of truth. Every thought comes with the punchline already built in, because that's how existence works: profoundly ridiculous, ridiculously profound, and impossible to escape.

What This Book Isn't

This is not philosophy trying to be entertaining. Nor is it self-help disguised as fulfillment, or a comedy that believes jokes alone can solve your problems. What follows is the real deal. Existential comedy is both the question and the answer. It's the recognition that we are all making it up as we go, that curiosity is both our compass and our cure, and that laughter might be the most honest response we have to the beautiful, terrible fact of our own existence. We are not making it easier. We're making it relevant, applying existentialism to the reality of human experience. What does it mean to be human, you may ask? The answer: awkward, mortal, confused, and from time to time, convinced the universe is breathing when it's just our own reflection staring back.

The Rules of Engagement

- Prioritize curiosity over being certain. Questions matter more than answers. As Albert Einstein said, "The important thing is not to stop questioning. Curiosity has its own reason for existing." The skull leans forward, always looking, never quite satisfied.

- Humor as Truth-Telling. If you can't laugh at the absurdity, you're missing half the point. Comedy reveals what philosophy can only explain. As Oscar Wilde noted, "If you want to tell people the truth, make them laugh, otherwise they'll kill you." Humor gives us a way to face life's contradictions, its chaos, and its cruelty while staying intact. The Body Knows. We carry our existentialism in our bones, our blood, and our breath. This isn't abstract theory. This is your actual life, happening in real time, inside a meat suit that is equal parts miracle and joke. As Clarissa Pinkola Estes writes in Women Who Run with the Wolves, "The body is the soul's house. Should the house fall, the soul will have to find a new one."

Your body knows. Listen to it, laugh with it, and let it guide you through the absurd.

- Embrace the both/and. Scholarly and silly. Rigorous and ridiculous. Meaning and meaningless. Grounded and groundlessness. The paradox is the point. Live through the wise words of Bruce Lee: "Empty your mind. Be formless, shapeless, like water. You put water into a cup; it becomes the cup. You put it into a bottle; it becomes the bottle. You put it into a teapot; it becomes the teapot. Now water can flow, or it can crash. Be water, my friend." In that flow, let each shape teach you how to live with curiosity, lightness, and laughter.

- No Pedestals or Soapboxes. Not for philosophers, not for gurus, not for anyone claiming they've figured it out. We are all in the same skeleton, trying to make sense of the inexplicable. As Elbert Hubbard famously said, "Do not take life too seriously. You will never get out of it alive." So lean into the bones, laughing at the absurd, and carry on: marrow-deep and unafraid.

Your Agreement

By continuing past this passage, you agree to:
- Question everyone, especially your own questions.

- Find humor in horror, lightness in darkness, and meaning in the void.

- Accept that existence is absurd and also beautiful, pointless and also precious.

- Laugh at yourself, with yourself, and about yourself.

- Carry your bones with curiosity, your heart with honesty, and your brain with a healthy dose of skepticism.

This is existential comedy. Philosophy in flesh and bone. The serious work of not taking ourselves too seriously. Life's autopsy while we're still alive.

Let's begin with the skull, shall we? It has questions.

THEMATIC SKELETON

Table of Contents

Bone #1 Skull of Curiosity 1
Existential Insert: The Cartilage 6
Bone #2 Jaws of Jabbering 9
Existential Insert: The Tongue 17
Bone #3 Funny Bone of Folly 19
Existential Insert: The Senses 23
Bone #4 Rib of Regret 25
Existential Insert: The Muscle 33
Bone #5 Spine of Stability 35
Existential Insert: The Limbic System 42
Bone #6 Collarbone of Connection 44
Existential Insert: The Organs 54
Bone #7 Femur of Fearlessness 56
Existential Insert: The Fat 65
Bone #8 Pelvis of Perspective 67
Existential Insert: The Arteries 75
Bone #9 The Stapes: Sound meets Sense 77
Existential Insert: The Nervous System 90
Bone #10 Metacarpal of Meaning 92

Existential Insert: The Skin 98
Bone #11 Metatarsals of Return 100
Existential Insert: The Soul 107
Bone #12 Humerus or Humorous 109
Life's A Punchline: Epilogue 118
Body of Evidence 120
Fingerprints 129

Being curious is why I studied forensic psychology and obsessed over death, only to leave the corpses for kitchens and classrooms, where the only thing I slice and dice is an opinion...and the occasional one-liner.

Life in Miniature: Curiosity at Home

I am currently compelled to observe life in miniature, a continuous source of fascination provided by my children. These tiny, paradoxical dictators negotiate bedtime as if it were international diplomacy. The wildly unreasonable things they say make me pause, laugh, and often question humanity itself. If I had a dime for every time I thought, "How did this tiny human come up with that?", I'd probably invest in a tiny, skeleton-themed cafe, serving existential dread alongside lattes.

Watching them, I notice minor details: the way a simple request to put their shoes on can launch a full-blown existential debate, or how a crayon scribble on the wall suddenly becomes a manifesto on color theory. Every question, every unexpected observation, feels like a window into a universe I did not know existed. Curiosity at home is relentless, contagious, and mostly uncontainable. This reminds me that even in the smallest corner of our lives, wonder waits patiently to be noticed, and sometimes it comes blaring like a foghorn.

How do you notice curiosity in your home?

Closing the Cranium of the Curious

In short, the skull of curiosity is never silent. Questions roam wildly, urging investigation and finding laughter in chaos. This is the first bone you examine in this comedic autopsy of existence. Without curiosity, a weak and delicate collection of bones would result from the skeletal structure, which includes the ribs that symbolize regret, the at the stillness while convinced she was breathing. I was in an instant mesmerized, horrified, and completely consumed. My chest rose and fell in perfect sync with what I thought was hers, and for a moment, I believed I had discovered the universe's hidden design.

That was my first lesson in existential comedy; life is absurd, death is literal, and your own chest may be the trickiest mirror of all. Sure, this was an unintentional performance, a debut in the theatre of existence, and the audience was terrifyingly silent. In the quiet atmosphere, the soft crying of those around me resonated; I didn't know then that they, too, were experiencing a moment of deep existential fear. Even now, I realize that moment planted a seed for a lifelong fascination with observing, questioning, and laughing at the strange spectacle of being alive.

Curiosity Through Life's Chaos

From childhood, I was always curious, as if a relentless voice within me urged me to notice, question, and explore everything. We are driven by curiosity to ask unusual questions, such as why we spend so much effort on predicting the future, given that it is inherently unpredictable. In what ways does the experience of scrolling through social media often feel akin to the action of ascending to a mountain's summit only to plunge directly into a chaotic whirlwind? Beyond that, and perhaps of the greatest importance, if I react to the ludicrous nature of everything with laughter, am I then reflecting on the fundamental nature of being, or am I just using my wit to postpone what is inescapable?

It is an undeniable fact that curiosity serves as a fundamental mechanism for our survival. It keeps us awake in the theater of reality, poking at the absurdities, shaking the curtain of our own assumptions, and reminding us there is always more to see, question, and enjoy.

Peering Through the Eye Sockets

Curiosity lives right behind the eyes, leaning forward to see everything while often missing the obvious. For centuries, humans have been questioning, why are we here? What is the point? And why does the universe seem to peek precisely when we're trying to sleep?

Curiosity does not ask; it nudges, it pokes, and offers counsel: Did I lock the door? Did I mess up that conversation? Should I go to the party? Curiosity's a pal, but also a bit of a tease, right? It leaves us in suspense, causing us to question our curiosity.

Albert Camus, a world-renowned philosopher and existentialist writer, argues that life is absurd: there's no inherent meaning, only that which we create. However, he lived and died before he could witness the true 21st-century absurdity: scrolling memes while pondering mortality. Regardless of the timeframe, the fundamental takeaway is constant: curiosity either redeems or amuses us.

Being curious inspires us to ask questions, chase ideas that make no practical sense, and now and then fall down rabbit holes we never intended to enter. Curiosity is an invisible energy that drives us to notice patterns in chaos, find humor in contradictions, and magnify the insignificant, like the existential weight of a single sock going missing. Camus recommended coming to terms with the absurd. I agree. Lean into the paradox with a smirk, a raised eyebrow, and if you like, a coffee in hand.

First Lessons in Existential Comedy

For me, curiosity started early–like, uncomfortably early. Picture a small child shoved in front of her grandmother's open casket, staring

BONE #1 SKULL OF CURIOSITY

Control center where absurdity meets insight

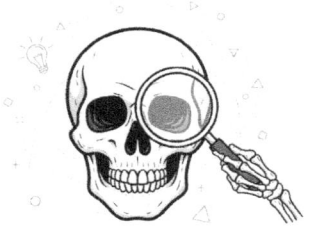

We should be clear before we begin the dissection. Curiosity is not a polite guest. It barges in, tilts your world sideways, and forces you to look closer at everything, even the things you'd rather ignore. The spark behind every question, a low hum in quiet moments, and drives the existential angst that makes us stop, wonder, and occasionally panic. Welcome to the Skull of Curiosity, the first bone in our comedic autopsy.

femurs that denote fearlessness, and the metacarpals that represent meaning, to name a few. Remember, curiosity is not optional. It's your front-row seat to the absurd theatre of being alive, your internal philosophical tour guide, and occasionally your very own ghost in the skull. Still curious? Let this be your guiding light to that which makes you human.

EXISTENTIAL INSERT: CARTILAGE

Bend without breaking

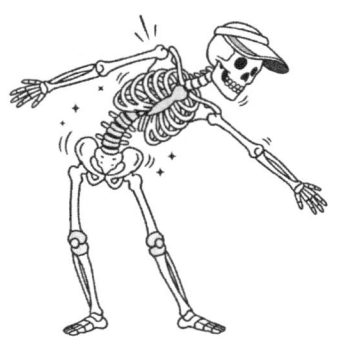

After most chapters, you'll hit a little "Existential Insert." Think of these as cartilage moments: the soft places between hard ideas, giving your brain a chance to stretch before something snaps. Don't worry, this isn't yoga. This page is your built-in pause, a breath in the middle of the book's skeleton, the place you get to look around before stepping onto the next bone and pretending you know what you're doing.

Curiosity wanders. Sometimes it hangs near the top of the skull while you dig through meaning like a cook hunting for the one ingredient that seems to vanish when needed most. Other times, curiosity camps out in the jaw, ready to clamp down with explanations, defenses, or that familiar compulsion to be right. Give the jaw a break. Nothing mystical here, just human maintenance. Let the hinge ease, the way it does right before a yawn. Did you yawn? If not, smile anyway. Maybe your body's reflexes were off today. Either way, the face has been performing, so a small release won't threaten your dignity.

This moment is not about enlightenment. The goal is to avoid bulldozing past your own thoughts. Philosophers have suggested for ages that questions behave better when you give them breathing room. Our minds do too. Meaning shows up in the gaps, those odd little pockets between ideas where the pressure drops and unexpected clarity emerges. A half-smile, a stray breath, a shoulder-drop: these slight shifts open the door more reliably than grappling with certainty. Sometimes the mind loosens like a joint, a gentle click, and then there's room to move again.

Practice: Catch yourself mid-opinion today. Before the usual rush to prove you're right, pause and ask, "What changes if I get curious instead of convinced?" Notice the changes: a drop in defensiveness, or a moment where your inner monologue insists on running the life show. Take this as a win; openness is its own regard. A single crack in certainty can let in more understanding than an entire day spent searching for answers.

You've just created a piece of existential cartilage: a small but dependable hinge between the ideas you've been chewing on and the ones ahead. Nothing to gnaw through here. This is a space to bend, breathe, and regroup. Curiosity wanders best when allowed to roam, not forced to march in cadence.

Daily Humor: Be like cartilage: flexible enough to keep everything moving, sturdy enough to take the pressure, and squeaky only when drama calls. A well-timed squeak can keep the whole day from going bone-on-bone. Remember: even cartilage needs comic relief.

BONE #2 JAWS OF JABBERING

From mumbling to meaning

As we turn our attention to the jaw, let us pause and consider the immense power it wields. This bone is more than a hinge for chewing; it serves as the launching pad for every sigh, question, rant, and punchline we have ever produced. Where curiosity meets expression, the jaw takes center stage–sometimes elegantly, sometimes clumsily, always boldly.

From whispering secrets to yelling at the kids to stop writing on the walls, the jaw is the body's original philosophical instrument. Welcome to the Jaws of Jabbering, the mouthful of meaning where thought meets speech, taste meets wit, and absurdity finds its voice. So open wide, let your thoughts spill out, and remember that even nonsense can carry its own kind of wisdom. Speak freely, for the mouth holds the stories of curiosity, and every word is a step forward, a little leap into self-discovery. Just as the jaw shapes our words, it also shapes the way we digest the world: bite by bite, syllable by syllable. The mandible carries the weight of every laugh, shout, and whispered secret. Pause for a moment, take a breath if you will, and let the chaos of expression settle before diving into this full spectacle.

The Mouthful of Meaning

The jawbone is more than bone; its muscle. The engine of every word, exhale, sarcastic comment, and unspoken thought, it's where curiosity meets expression and often collides seamlessly with chaos. Since the beginning of time, or at least as far back as anyone can remember, humans have jabbered about everything from the cosmos to their neighbor's peculiar habits, often with the same intensity as Socrates and Plato debating virtue, except now with more emojis.

Communication can be a glorious cacophony of voices, sometimes absurd and other times utterly terrifying. We speak to connect, to impress, to negotiate, and occasionally just to fill the silence when we are unsure of what we truly feel. The jaw, a philosopher's original tool, opens and closes, chews on ideas, and sometimes gets carried away with more than we can put into words.

For me, the mouth became a conduit for my culinary life. In the kitchen, words and tastes are inseparable. The mandible is always active, conveying directions, experiencing flavors, exposing the tastes of existence, modulating, and exchanging witty remarks with coworkers and customers. It does more than speak; it tastes, it savors, and it shapes experience. Every slice, every bite, every perfectly timed punchline in a thoughtfully cooked dish mirrors the same precision and audacity as words delivered with wit.

Chattering Philosophers

If you think humans are the first to ramble absurdly about existence, think again!, Plato wrote dialogues, and somewhere in ancient Greece, someone likely turned a dinner symposium into a full-blown debate over whether water or wine was the true elixir of wisdom. For ages, philosophers have relied on the jaw for their heavy lifting, from posing questions, offering answers, or simply evoking the ever-so subtle eye-roll of their neighbors.

Fast-forward a few millennia and the chatter continues, only now with more emojis, memes, and nearly 300-character existential texts. Camus dismissed life's absurd nature with a shrug; Nietzsche cautioned that the impact of language is greater than its meaning. Yet both understood a truth every chef, parent, and over-caffeinated philosopher eventually learns: timing is of the essence. A poorly timed word may ruin a dinner, a joke, a relationship, or even a spot-on lecture about absurdism.

I have noticed that many of my philosophical musings still arrive in the kitchen, even just making dinner at home. Knife in hand or stirring a simmering pot, I reflect on the absurdity of what it means to be human. Picture this: I am dicing an onion, tears flowing down my face. Shocked, my little one stands in the paradox of being: "Why is mommy crying in the kitchen?" I tell her, "The onion and its many layers make you cry, but it's not as tragic as existence itself." She tilts her head, gives a Camus-like shrug, and goes back to playing; sweetly and unknowingly displaying the masterful art of acknowledging the absurd that is being.

My mom always said her mother told her, "The farmers must have been mad when they planted the onions" because of how they make us cry. Over the years, I have wondered how many peaceful farmers exist, since I can count on one hand the number of times I haven't cried cutting onions. Keep the root intact, use a sharp knife, keep the onions cold, chew gum or eat bread while chopping–everyone has a trick, and the list goes on. But not to wander too far off course, words flow, flavors unfold, and laughter bubbles up. It is a fitting metaphor for the jaw in action: speaking, chewing, tasting, making a mess, and shedding a tear over an onion. In these moments, I almost feel a mischievous wink from Nietzsche himself, as if he's whispering from the pantry, "Yes, cry your onions, but remember, tears are just the seasoning for the soul."

Personal Jabbering

More often than I care to admit, my jaw moves faster than my brain. I launch into stories about existential dread while explaining why the refrigerator is a metaphor for hope. One of the most influential thinkers of the 20th century, Ludwig Wittgenstein, might approve–or at least roll his eyes. There's a certain chaos to personal expression, a push and pull between thought and speech, where a sentence may be both brilliant and ridiculous, and words themselves carry meaning.

Succinctly, the jaw is where curiosity finds its voice. We articulate our reflections, our absurdities, and the little tangents that reveal our humanity with our mandibles. This is our mouthpiece for chaos, our delivery system for punchlines, and our emotional echo chamber. It is the place where insight and nonsense collide, where ideas taste the air before they land, and where rhythm of thought meets the texture of speech.

The Jabbering at Home

Our mouths have the dual ability to spark intellectual conversations or playful banter near the fridge, while also contributing to household disarray. At my home, my mandibles hardly ever rest.

The kids also figured out the answers to life's big questions–the why, how, when, where, and what–while settling arguments over toys and creating their own stories, often fueled by snacks and casual chats. Did I mention why? After years in professional kitchens, I sometimes joke that I'm a short-order cook at home, now serving questions instead of orders and teaching these little souls the meaning of life between peanut-butter sandwiches. Isn't this what life is about? Searching for meaning while buttering bread?

Children, after all, are born existentialists. They speak without hesitation about life's biggest mysteries. Some of my preschoolers' questions have thrown me for a loop: Where does blood come from? How are babies made? What does our heart look like? When are we going to die? What is gay? Was I in your tummy? Why is the moon following us in the car? Why does the sun disappear at night?

These questions arrive at full volume with no warning. The jaw pivots fast–every mandible in the room ready for questions. One moment we are explaining the illogical end of being to a child holding an ice cream sandwich; the next I'm kneading pizza dough while pondering mortality.

Domestic blabber has a rhythm of its own. It's a call and response of domestic philosophy, heightened by spilled juice and the ricochet of kids at full speed. Home is where my mouth does its greatest work: testing patience, shaping humor, and confronting meaninglessness in a language little beings can almost understand.

Sometimes, amid the unfiltered questions and commentary, I slip into a full kitchen-sink monologue. Plato in pajama pants, Socrates with a spatula. The kitchen table becomes a forum, and the living room an impromptu debate hall. Unlike the halls of academia, our arguments end with giggles, hugs, or someone asking for another ice cream sandwich.

At home, the jaw is at its most human. Not just chewing food or forming words, but creating connection. Talking at home reminds me that speech is not only for explaining but for weaving tiny threads of meaning between people. Every question answered, every punchline delivered, every offhand comment builds a shared story.

In this way, even the smallest chatter carries wisdom. Life's absurdities meet you with curiosity, and maybe a crumb or stain on your shirt—a stain of meaning. From the clatter of dishes and the ruckus of preschool questions to the Moscow teahouses and the halls of academia, the jaw has always been a tool for chewing on meaning and laughing at existence.

Mouthfuls of Humor

The jawbone has always been a powerful instrument. In the right hands, words can build civilizations. Humor has long been philosophy's secret sidekick. For every serious treatise on despair, there's a witty note on the absurd.

Soren Kierkegaard, the father of existentialism, wrote of "the sickness unto death," while also understanding irony to remain upright in a crooked world. Building on Kierkegaard, Jean-Paul Sartre filled Parisian cafes with ideas about freedom and nausea while tossing off one-liners sharp enough to cut through the cigarette smoke wafting through the air of the era. Even the existential feminist Simone de Beauvoir, while mapping the ethics of ambiguity, sprinkled her prose with sly wit. Laughter doesn't erase the void; it makes it breathable.

Across the centuries, the mouth has acted as a philosophical hinge between tragedy and comedy. We chew bread, and we wrestle with paradoxes. In challenging times, smirking at life's absurdities illuminates the resilient light of humor. Camus's "absurd man," confronted with the meaninglessness of existence, may have grinned at the spectacle of being in time. Nietzsche wielded humor like a tool, chipping away at rigid morals with cosmic punchlines. Philosophers have long woven jokes and clever imagery into their thinking, moving monumental ideas without crushing the human experience under the weight of existence.

In those moments of deep thought, maybe we'll take a break to eat, chuckle, and wish life had a guidebook. Today, the stage for existential humor is less the Roman Colosseum or a London pub and more the everyday spaces where life unfolds: grocery lines, office break rooms, and the dinner table. People still quote philosophers, but now it's more common on coffee mugs, t-shirts, and memes. The jaw has developed beyond its initial purpose of survival; every quip about existence, no matter how complex, is part of an ancestral tradition of pondering the universe and laughing at the falling crumbs.

Next time you find yourself mid-sentence, pondering life's absurdity over frozen peas in aisle seven, remember you're always in excellent company. Camus may smirk at the shelves, Nietzsche may wink from a cereal box, and Sartre would likely remind you that even this moment is entirely of your own choosing. I cannot help but wonder what cereal would be in a box featuring Nietzsche winking. Another of life's absurd moments, to savor with a grin.

Closing the Mandible of Meaning

The jaw also performs functions beyond simply chewing food; it chews on ideas, jokes, and the paradoxes of life. We remember reflection and laughter often go together, from preschool questions at the kitchen table to Nietzsche winking from a cereal box. Even in chaos, a well-timed word, a shared pun, a twist of a meme, or an unspoken smirk can make the weight of existence feel lighter.

The mandible is part philosopher, part trickster, delivering insight, levity, and occasional mischief in equal measure. It's both our instrument of thought and our vehicle for connection, guiding us through the absurdity of life one syllable at a time.

Considering this jaw-dropping information, the next time your mouth is full of words, food, or laughter, embrace its power. Every question, witty remark, or exhale is a tiny act of connection, a slight rebellion against meaninglessness, and a chance to savor life's absurd celestial crumbs.

EXISTENTIAL INSERT: THE TONGUE

That slippery muscle between truth and taste

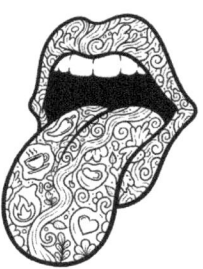

The tongue is a slippery muscle, juggling flavor, feeling, apology, and appetite all at once. Tongues charm, wound, and confuse while making fools of us at high speed. Every slip, hesitation, and measured word proves perfection is a myth. You cannot fake paying attention. Our mistakes and the messes we make all hold meaning.

Tongues teach patience in the most humiliating ways. They force us to pay attention to how we taste and speak in the world. Words stumble, vowels vanish, and you become the comedian, the punchline, and the roast victim. Vulnerability shows up in tongue-tied moments, Freudian slips, and awkward pauses that make everyone stare at you as if you just fell into a live broadcast of someone else's horror show.

Practice: Say something true but unnecessary out loud. A confession, an absurd complaint, or a ridiculous observation. Watch your tongue twist, stumble, and go overboard, as if auditioning for a sitcom. Sit with the embarrassment, then laugh at the absurdity. Let your body betray you: jaw tension, stomach butterflies, and the relief when the words finally land. Precision is irrelevant. Presence is everything.

Daily Humor: Every slip, mangled truth, and improvised punchline is a free comedy show. You might make someone laugh, groan, or question their life choices. No schedule, no rehearsals, no mercy. The chaos is always worth savoring and often tastes better than most carefully prepared meals. Remember: if your tongue slips, let it be—applause is optional.

BONE #3 FUNNY BONE OF FOLLY

Life is serious enough; laughter is mandatory

If the jaw is the philosopher's tool, the funny bone is its mischievous sidekick. This is where life's absurdities catch us by surprise here–tripping over our own feet, sending a text to the wrong person, or realizing mid-sentence that you've been quoting Sigmund Freud instead of Carl Jung...again. The funny bone does more than provoke laughter; it reminds us that foolishness is an essential part of being human. This truth often humbles us when we bump our funny bone, eyes tearing up as a sharp jolt of pain reminds us that discomfort is also a part of the human condition. Welcome to the Funny Bone of Folly. We kindly request that you keep your arms within the ride at all times and uphold your dignity during the duration of the ride.

Philosophy in Laughter

Humor is more than a flurry of giggles–it's philosophy in action. Kierkegaard, wrestling with dread and the existential anxiety of freedom, understood irony as a way of keeping the self from faltering under the weight of life. Existential thinker Viktor Frankl, even amid the horrors of the Holocaust, observed that finding meaning through small moments of levity could preserve the soul. Another renowned existentialist, Rollo May, argued that courage and playfulness are inseparable; to come face-to-face with the void, we must sometimes laugh at the illusion of space first. Simone de Beauvoir, while dissecting the ethics of ambiguity, still allowed her wit to slip through the cracks of her rigorous prose. Laughter, like an unseen muscle, stretches and strengthens us against the pressure of being in the world.

The funny bone itself is a bodily emblem of this truth. A bump or shock produces an immediate, visceral response–a laugh or wince–that reminds us we are alive, unpredictable, and fragile. When we fall, gesture wildly, or shrug at life's absurdities, our bodies perform unspoken comedy. Humor allows us to experiment with identity, question authority, and explore the tension between freedom and limitation. Sartre's nausea meets the slapstick of tripping over a rug, and Camus' absurd finds its sparring partner in a seagull stealing your lunch mid-bite. The existential mind may dwell on the ultimate questions, but the body insists on immediate, sometimes ridiculous, answers.

Surely, the funny bone teaches humility. Pain and laughter often coexist, and even the most profound insight can arrive through a stumble, a misstep, or a shared joke. In classrooms, kitchens, playgrounds, at dinner tables, this bone prods us to find comfort in the unpredictable, to embrace folly as a part of wisdom. Every jolt, every unexpected reaction, carries a lesson. To live fully is to lean into the absurd, to honor the body's wisdom, and to allow humor to illuminate the darkest corners of existence.

Everyday Theatre of Foolishness

Even today, the theater of human folly plays out in the most mundane settings. The car refuses to start, a child hides the house keys, someone misquotes a song lyric at a party, and suddenly we remember that laughter is not a distraction but a survival skill. The funny bone, in all its brilliance, teaches that comedy is a lens through which we may examine freedom, responsibility, the absurd, and even mortality—without succumbing to the weight of angst.

Ultimately, the funny bone reminds us that life does not take itself too seriously at every turn. Life is a patient teacher, showing us how to find lightness amid gravity, recognize the absurd in everyday moments, and honor the body as much as the mind in our pursuit of meaning. A stubbed toe, a misfired joke, or spilled milk becomes more than a minor mishap. These follies are invitations to laugh, to connect, and to embrace the wonderfully imperfect human experience. Humor is not an escape from existence; it's a way to inhabit it to the fullest.

Look closely, and you'll see the funny bone's lessons spilling into every corner of life. The kitchen timer screams, the laundry creates chaos, a punchline lands awkwardly in conversation, and these events remind us that meaning often appears with gaffes, falls, and minor disasters. Each moment of absurdity is a breadcrumb leading to awareness, an appetizer for curiosity, and sometimes a side of existential seasoning.

So as we prepare to explore the next chapter, the Rib of Regret, remember this: the funny bone has done its work. It has loosened our tension, sharpened our attention to the absurd, and coaxed a sneer from the corners of our minds. Holding onto that sense of mischief is essential, as regret can be a heavy burden, and humor provides the most effective means of handling that weight with ease.

EXISTENTIAL INSERT: THE SENSES

Your five senses, now with existential seasoning

The senses are our first, most relentless, and mischievous teachers. Sight lies, hearing exaggerates, taste betrays, touch confuses, and smell never lets you forget what's present. All our overreactions and misperceptions are proof humans come with built-in punchlines. We stumble through life, attempting to interpret reality, only to discover that our own perceptions are the main comedy. Life's purpose might hide in the minor flaws: past mistakes, strange smells, or even the tastes of success.

Our senses are relentless guides, challenging our assumptions. A shadow in the corner may startle us, a sudden gust of wind may rearrange our hair–and our thoughts, and a song on repeat can feel both comforting and absurd. Every sensory encounter is a chance to pause and marvel at the difference between expectation and reality. By paying attention to the unexpected, we train ourselves to notice the humor in the ordinary. The world becomes a stage where sight, sound, taste, touch, and smell conspire to surprise, provoke, and often embarrass us–a reminder that life is never as serious as we imagine.

Practice: Pick a sense and watch it sabotage you today. Smell the coffee, the trash, the outside air, and give each an absurd name. Touch a countertop, a shoe, a wall and invent a secret life story for each. Listen to a dripping faucet, a car horn, your own voice and cast every sound in a tragedy. Taste something ordinary or ridiculous and declare yourself a revolutionary chef. Watch the body react: surprise, disgust, delight, existential horror. Laugh at the absurdity of existing.

Daily Humor: Sight, sound, touch, taste, smell conspiring to prove control is a myth. The spice misfires, a texture revolts, a sound deceives. These senses stage a comedy of errors with you as both audience and punchline. Lean into the chaos. Laugh anyway. Remember: if life hands you a rotten tomato, throw it at a wall and call it contemporary art. No tomatoes suffered while crafting this advice.

BONE #4 RIB OF REGRET

Regret: The ghost with a funny hat

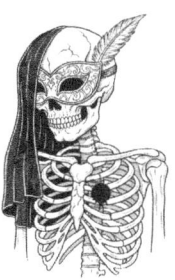

Regret is an oddly intimate companion, lingering at the edge of our choices and acting as a shadowy witness to the paths we took, the words we spoke, and the chances we let slip away. Philosophers, including notable figures like Kierkegaard and Sartre, have devoted considerable thought to the complex nature of regret, recognizing it as an inevitable outcome of our freedom, and understanding its connection to the struggle between our decisions and the options we don't pursue. Yet regret often carries a hint of the ridiculous. Life reminds us that being human comes with a mix of reflection, nonsense, madness, and missed opportunities. The haunting what-ifs remain long after the moment has passed. Welcome to the Rib of Regret, the only bone where past mistakes come seasoned with irony and a side of "I really shouldn't have done that."

The Haunting What-Ifs

Regret is never content to stay hidden. It appears uninvited, often at the most inconvenient moments. Imagine sitting at a red light, daydreaming about a new date, when suddenly, a what-if hits you with the subtlety of a brick wall. How would things have changed if you had spoken differently at dinner? What if you had raised your hand in the morning meeting? Had you boarded the plane to New Orleans before the hurricane's winds claimed the streets? What if you had exercised more before or eaten dessert later? The what-ifs are relentless visitors, part philosopher, part trickster, twisting ordinary choices into existential dilemmas. Kierkegaard, who wrestled with anxiety and choice, might nod knowingly here. He described our freedom as both a gift and a burden, a constant confrontation with possibility. Each what-if echoes our endlessly choosing, endlessly responsible, and endlessly human nature.

In reality, these hauntings of regret rarely stay abstract. They show up in little, persistent ways: a friendship that drifted apart, a missed career opportunity, or a word left unsaid to a loved one. Sartre framed this as the weight of freedom, where every choice we make carries infinite consequences. I feel it most in quiet moments—taking a shower, folding laundry, driving, stirring a pot—when the mind drifts to paths untraveled. There's an absurdity to it all. Camus would probably smile at the mental gymnastics we perform, treating missed opportunities as tragedies of epic proportion while the world carries on. Even Frankl, who endured unimaginable suffering, understood the value of perspective: meaning can exist even in the haunting what-ifs that follow us.

Modern existential thinkers like Rollo May give this cosmic dance a practical edge. Regret is a teacher, not a punishment. It illuminates our values, our desires, and the choices we risked, ignored, or avoided. I see this in my life as well, from parenting to friendships to career moves. The what-ifs are persistent, yet they keep me alert and engaged. Simone de Beauvoir observed that a fully lived life involves a constant negotiation between choices, consequences, and recognition of our inevitable limits. Yet, for all of my philosophical insight, I still can't figure out why socks disappear in the laundry.

Humor, as always, sneaks into the forest of regret, a sly fox among the shadows. There's a ridiculousness in imagining what life could have been if we had taken every path. Picture the alternate you, standing in the rain, juggling three backpacks, explaining to the Lyft driver why you became a pastry chef instead of a forensic pathologist. The mind can be both cruel and comical, turning existential reflection into an open-mic set. Nietzsche might chime in from a metaphorical seat in the audience, reminding us that even the weight of regret has form, texture, and demands ironic acknowledgment.

Ultimately, the haunting what-ifs are inseparable from existence itself. They arrive unannounced, linger like shadows, and sometimes make us wince, laugh, or both at the same time. The challenge is to engage, not escape, regret. Let the missteps, abandoned dreams, and offhand words guide you, with seriousness and absurd laughter, toward the choices that remain before you. Life insists that the what-ifs exist, and humor, reflection, and a dash of self-compassion help determine how much attention they deserve.

Lessons in Hindsight

Hindsight is less of a nagging guest and more of a sly teacher, arriving after the chaos with a knowing look and a notebook full of observations. It highlights the absurdity of our regrettable actions and inactions. Kierkegaard would call this the anxiety of choice meeting the comedy of error. Sartre would remind us we are always responsible, even for our ridiculous blunders. The lesson is obvious: reflecting on the past reveals patterns, but also highlights the sheer theater of human life. It also exposes the subtle humor embedded in our attempts to journey through the odyssey of existence.

We also see what we almost did: the doors we hesitated to open, the jokes we never told, or the awkward silences we could have filled with courage or nonsense. Frankl would argue that meaning exists in the choices we make today, but hindsight offers the privilege of perspective. We can laugh at the extremes of our youthful self-seriousness. We can marvel at how the small, seemingly insignificant moments shape us. Considering the world's constant development, and its disregard for our minor tragedies, even Camus may express bewilderment at the lengths we go to in order to dramatize our past.

The humor in hindsight is significant. Nietzsche would likely applaud the irony in how often we take ourselves too seriously–only to appreciate the foolishness years later when we recount the story over coffee. The things we once feared or fretted over–embarrassments, misunderstandings, and awkward choices–become fuel for laughter, empathy, and insight. Hindsight teaches that existence is not just about the weight of regret or the haunting of what-ifs. It is also about the joy of noticing our own absurdity, embracing it, and moving forward with a light step, ready to encounter the next laughable twist in the unfolding play of life. Or at the very least, it teaches us that spilling coffee on our own shirt is always funnier in retrospect.

Laughing in the Abyss

It's an unusual freedom that comes from staring into the emptiness, and rather than being afraid, you laugh. The abyss has long served as a metaphor for confronting the unknown. Kierkegaard wrote of anxiety, Sartre of nothingness, and Heidegger explored the "possibility of the impossibility of any existence at all." Irvin Yalom described the four ultimate concerns—death, freedom, isolation, and meaninglessness—and noted that facing death honestly can let humor loosen its grip.

It's one thing to read about dread, but quite another to realize you are staring into the abyss while waiting for coffee, mulling over that awkward message you sent two days ago. In that moment, the void is not a distant galaxy but a familiar space where regret and self-awareness meet, and a well-timed laugh becomes a lifeline.

Psychologist Carl Jung believed that the parts of ourselves we push away are not only dark but also playful, acting as inner jokers. To laugh into the abyss is to make eye contact with your own shadow and see it grinning back. Heidegger would likely frown at the thought, but even he acknowledged that authentic existence involves facing anxiety without disguise. Humor doesn't erase our anxiety; it gives us a way to breathe while we stand in the angst. The abyss is heavy, yet laughter can create buoyancy—like throwing a whoopee cushion into a black hole.

I have found this to be true in the most ordinary moments. A failed recipe, a forgotten appointment, a breakup, or a poorly timed apology are my mini-abysses. While they are not tragedies, they feel that way at the moment. Whether I am telling a friend about it at a later time or just thinking about it, I always end up laughing. That laugh is not dismissal; it's acknowledgment. It's my psyche, in Jung's sense, integrating what felt unbearable into something human–and even a little funny. Laughing in the abyss becomes less an act of denial and more an act of courage. This is my way of standing on the edge, looking down, and waving into the darkness rather than recoiling from its truth. Try it!

Shared Shadows

If Jung saw the shadow as a private underworld, he also recognized that it never stays entirely private. Our shadows leak into relationships–through jokes, irritations, Freudian slips, resentments, and unguarded honesty. Heidegger wrote about "being-with" as an essential feature of existence, and this is where our shadows become social. Sometimes, the people closest to me carry pieces of my integrated self, just as I carry theirs. In this sense, every friendship, every romance, every family gathering becomes an informal shadow exchange program.

There's something oddly consoling about shared shadows. Sharing softens the blow of facing death, freedom, and isolation, as Yalom points out. Even a dark confession can feel lighter when spoken aloud; a private regret becomes weightless when someone else acknowledges, "Me too." Humor plays a subtle role, not to belittle, but as a mutual wink across the abyss. When two people can laugh at their shared follies, they also acknowledge a shared humanity. This is the alchemy of shared shadows: what once felt shameful or isolating becomes a bond.

Shared shadows can be delightfully absurd. I've laughed at the ridiculousness of collective anxieties–panicking over losing our phone while it's actually in your hand. In these small, comical mishaps, existential truth hides. We are all fumbling through life, juggling regret, fear, and the occasional chocolate craving, hoping no one notices how little control we really have. Should someone notice, the moment becomes even funnier as we laugh together, standing in the dark and holding each other's metaphorical flashlights. Sometimes the best philosophical insight comes wrapped in a simple punchline: we are all humans misplacing phones, thoughts, and dignity from time to time.

Ribs Reclaimed

Reclaiming your ribs means reclaiming the breath you forgot you were holding. Beneath the rhetorical rib cage sit your lungs, instinctive and unthinking, expanding and collapsing whether you notice. They are living proof that while the ribs can form a cage, your life does not need to feel confined. Every regret, every what-if, every shadow and lingering anxiety clings on to you like an app you cannot delete from your phone. This is the moment to swipe it away, feel the space it leaves in your chest, and remember that you are more than a collection of missed opportunities. You are still breathing, still laughing, still able to move forward. Existential psychologist Kirk Schneider calls this capacity for awe "a vital antidote to disconnection," beginning with small moments of noticing your lungs swell and your ribs open with each breath. It's a reminder that you're still here, reclaiming space in your own body.

There's power in laughing at the self you once were–not to criticize, but to reclaim. Epictetus observes that self-reflection carries its own amusement: noticing our foibles ensures life never runs out of moments to laugh at ourselves. Imagine all the ways your past self failed or stumbled. Now envision lifting those moments, one by one, and placing them in the light like a collection of mini-trophies. There's freedom in seeing those regrets as real but also comical. The chest expands not only with air but with acknowledgment, the realization that the absurdity of our foolishness is a sign of a life well attempted. Some missteps may even be a blessing in disguise.

Reclaiming your ribs also honors the human capacity to carry the weight of existence while reveling in the discovery of being. Humor becomes resistance, a way of showing the void that you are both present and untamed. Even Carl Jung would smile at the idea of coaxing our shadows, which were long thought to be serious and dark, into winking at us from within our own ribcages. Each laugh, every admission of error, strengthens your existential muscles, reminding you that while the ribs protect, they do not confine. Your breath, your laughter, your presence are living proof of resilience.

At last, reclaiming your ribs is a practice in standing taller and trusting the strength beneath you–the spine. Each inhale affirms the support you already possess, every laugh eases the tension of what is past, and every minor act of awareness confirms that you are upright, capable, and ready. You are ready to meet the Spine of Stability and carry both the weight and joy of being present after reclaiming the ribs and opening the chest. Ribs reclaimed and in charge, you can flex like a bodybuilder at a philosophy convention or giggle at your own internal whoopee cushion–because even existential muscles deserve a little mischief.

EXISTENTIAL INSERT: THE MUSCLE

Gravity bites; humor heals

Muscles do more than move the body. They carry tension, effort, and sometimes the memory of every awkward, regretful, or absurd moment you've endured. Muscles have a memory. Likewise, your existential muscles strengthen each time you stumble, confront regret, or laugh into the void. Stretching them is not about perfection. It's about acknowledging the burden you hold, sensing it, and appreciating that both the body and mind are far more resilient than you might expect.

These muscles also hold the capacity for joy, spontaneity, and surprise. Every smile, every burst of laughter, and playful motion flexes a part of you that language cannot capture. They form the hidden framework that lets you embrace living, recover from mistakes, and rise after setbacks with humility and humor. Exercising these muscles is not only a way to lighten your load, but more importantly, a method to celebrate the absurdity and richness of being human.

Practice: Pick a muscle and make it do something out of character. Flex your shoulders like you are shrugging off a lifetime of poor choices. Lift your arms as if you are hoisting one awkward conversation, one embarrassing thought, or one ridiculous regret over your head. Twist, reach, and overdo it like the star of a slapstick workout video. Watch your body react: tension, surprise, a little pride, maybe even a snort of laughter. Pretend your existential muscles are laughing with you, ready to carry the next absurd tumble, the next misstep, the next cosmic joke.

Daily Humor: Flex the body, flex the spirit, and make the absurd a part of your routine. Lift regrets like dumbbells. Curl worries like spaghetti. Press nonsense to your chest and exhale with exaggerated flair. Every clumsy gesture and outrageous stretch is repetition in the absurd gym of life. Your existential muscles are now ripped, limber, and prepared for the next comedic curveball. Laugh. Fall. Repeat. Remember: if you hit yourself in the face while flexing, consider this avant-garde performing art.

BONE #5 SPINE OF STABILITY

Perfect posture, same chaos

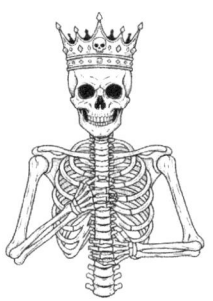

Life can feel like a game of Jenga on a rollercoaster, with the spine acting as the essential support to prevent everything from crashing. More than just a stack of bones, literally and metaphorically, the spine bears witness to every tilt, tumble, misstep, and unexpected twist. Without it, you would collapse, flexing, swaying, and cracking while insisting, "Yes, I'm holding this together, even if you are not." Welcome to the Spine of Stability, your personal stack of courage, chaos, and comic relief.

Finding Your Center

Finding your center is less about sitting cross-legged in meditation and more about realizing your core has been swaying like a toddler learning to walk all along. Rollo May suggested that courage is not the absence of fear; it's the act of dancing with it, anyway. This dance often feels like holding your backbone straight while juggling doubt and existential dread at the same time. Thinkers across the ages have struggled with the tension between chaos and composure, and none pretended life was tidy. The ancient Greeks called this Sophrosyne, the balance of mind, body, and soul–though I suspect they also contended with rancid olives and neighbors yelling at the toga party next door.

Humor is your best stabilizer. As you stumble toward equilibrium, laugh at the absurdity of being human. Tripping over yourself trying to "find your center," misquoting a Stoic to colleagues, or watching a profound thought get interrupted by a jet breaking the sound barrier, all become fountains of unexpected, youthful laughter. Perhaps it's the closest we will ever come to the fountain of youth. Rollo May might say these small failures are where creativity and courage intersect. Sartre would glare and remind you that you are always free to choose: free to stumble, free to spill milk, or free to laugh at the mess. Life presses down like the world's heaviest sweater, yet it gives your spine reason to flex and your lungs a purpose to exhale with laughter.

Centering is both an art and an experiment. Jung might suggest looking at your shadow and counting your absurdities as part of the equation. Epicurus might suggest enjoying wine and dessert for a balanced life, as he believed that without pleasure, existence is just polite suffering. Ever practical, May would urge you to notice, breathe, and commit to the messy dance of existence, anyway. Still, nothing tests philosophy like juggling parenting, client meal prep, and deadlines while pretending to have mastered mindfulness. If enlightenment does not arrive, at least dinner will.

Stand, sway, laugh, inhale the chaos, exhale the guilt, and let the body show the mind that stability is not perfection. Being stable means embracing the nonsensical, the joyful, and the terrifying in one graceless yet glorious pose. From here, we move into the weight of being, where your newly discovered center meets the gravity of choice, consequence, and all the outlandish responsibility that comes with simply existing.

The Weight of Being

The weight of being is anything but subtle. It presses down like a stack of overdue library books on your chest, clarifying that being human comes with obligations, mistakes, and the universe's particular brand of irony. In his work, Rollo May referred to this as the "gravity of existence." Even ancient philosophers wrestled with this truth, though they had fewer emails to answer. Your spine, your literal backbone, bears this weight every day, a testament that standing upright is itself an act of courage. For those whose bodies or lives won't let them stand today, know that even the smallest effort to rise, breathe, or persist is no less brave.

Humor is our essential counterbalance. Laughing at life's ridiculousness, such as the bills, deadlines, and accidental text messages sent to the wrong person, is not denial; it is survival. Nietzsche might whisper that to endure the burden of existence, we must sometimes dance with the absurd. We let the rain soak through our being and know that we are alive. Your spine is strong, but without humor, it risks bowing to the spectacle of reality. Allow yourself to sway, chuckle, and let the day shift beneath your balance. Each laugh is a mild mutiny against the heaviness of being.

Weight is not only a burden; it's also a signal drawing attention to what truly matters, what we carry willingly, and what we desperately wish to set down. According to Heidegger, "being-toward-death" gives life its shape, and within that shape, meaning emerges. Despite everything, it's still possible to say that the universe possesses a sense of humor. The real comedy is balancing love, work, fear, and joy all at once, while trying to step off the LEGOs of life.

Flexibility Within Structure

Even the sturdiest spine needs to bend. Life does not hand out a straight manual, and your vertebrae are proof that strength alone is not enough; adaptability matters just as much. Consider resilience a dance between endurance and pliability. Rollo May shows us that resilience is fluid, stretching, contracting, and flowing through uncertainty. Reflecting an existential truth, the human spine showcases its segmented magnificence.

Humor remains a critical stabilizer. Picture this: you've committed to standing or sitting tall amid life's chaos, only to have your posture interrupted by spilled coffee, a child's improvised dance, or your own optimistic interpretation of a Stoic maxim. Life offers a quirky union of wisdom: Horace's Carpe diem urges you to seize the day, while Nietzsche's Amor Fati challenges you to embrace whatever comes. Or if you prefer a modern twist, Carpe Fati–seize your fate–reminds you to accept joy, chaos, or even spilled coffee with equal gusto. Together, these maxims encourage you to stand tall, yield when necessary, and find humor in life's contradictions. Flexibility allows you to survive these interruptions without unraveling into existential despair, turning every failure into a lesson in courage and unexpected laughter. Jung would likely say that facing your shadow is not about avoidance; it is about welcoming life's absurdities and recognizing them in yourself. Even your most awkward shortcomings become teachable moments, stretching the spine and the spirit.

Adaptability is not only for those who can physically stand tall. For anyone weaving through illness, injury, or bodily limitations, true agility comes from discovering a spine of stability within mind and breath. You may not bend easily, but your consciousness, humor, and curiosity can still pivot and sway, absorbing life's twists and turns. The moments of joy, discovery, and simply being there contribute significantly to the core strength that you possess within yourself. Ultimately, fortitude is less about the shape of your body and more about the shape of your engagement with existence, preparing you to uncover the inner strength and audacity that hold us upright even in life's heaviest moments. With this foundation, we are ready to meet the backbone of courage, where daring, adaptability, and existential bravery converge.

The Backbone of Courage

Courage is rarely the stuff of grand gestures. More often, it's the backbone that straightens when no one is watching. Rollo May insisted that bravery is often just the will to move despite the angst. When we face the unknown, like sending a vulnerable text, speaking our mind in a crowd, or admitting a fault, we are flexing a vertebra of bravery. Our spines, both physical and symbolic, hold us upright, even when our thoughts spin like a carousel out of control.

Still, courage is as much comedic as it is noble. Consider spilling coffee on a crisp white shirt before an important meeting, or mispronouncing the speaker's name at a TED Talk. These petty acts of audacity, embarrassing as they may feel, remind us that courage does not require flawlessness. Sartre might observe that freedom carries responsibility and absurd consequences; every tiny act of daring is a testament to our persistent, ridiculous, authentic human being.

The backbone of courage is collectivity. Bravery thrives in shared laughter and mutual recognition of our botched attempts to be seen. Even the smallest bit of validation when we admit defeat reinforces the invisible vertebra of valor. The spine is no longer just a symbol of personal fortitude; it is a structure supporting connection, creativity, and presence. Each fearless act we commit, big or small, becomes a link in a chain of boldness that stretches from our own internal core to the paths we cross and the lives we touch.

Aligned for Life

Alignment is not about standing perfectly still, nor about achieving perfection. It's the ongoing negotiation between our inner values and external choices, the hilarious tragedy of being alive. When your backbone supports you, decisions feel lighter, laughter comes more freely, and your breath deepens. Rollo May might call this courage in motion, and Kierkegaard recognize the tension of choice. Life becomes less of a tightrope and more of a dance, full of missteps, unpredictable turns, and the occasional stumble.

Humor continues to stabilize us, showing that rigid rules do not build alignment. Being aligned for life means cultivating a stance that welcomes connection, courage, and the ease of following where life leads. The awareness, flexibility, and strength honed along our path extend outward, like branches from a rooted tree–the spinal column of nature itself. In keeping with our existential anatomy, we now turn to the Collarbone of Connection, where alignment becomes relational, and the movement of our ribs, shoulders, and arms reflects the ways we reach toward one another.

EXISTENTIAL INSERT: THE LIMBIC SYSTEM

THE PUPPET MONSTER YOU NEVER ASKED TO MEET

Limbic system structures deep in the brain regulate emotion, memory, and behavior, with the amygdala and hippocampus helping us respond to the world and survive. Imagine an inner volcano, bubbling with feelings, instincts, and questionable decisions. In this space, love was born, fear took root, and the saddest stories found their voices. While alarm bells from the amygdala ring, the hippocampus reruns childhood embarrassments. Somehow, we mistake this emotional turbulence for identity.

Here's the existential twist: the limbic system is dramatic. Built for survival, not serenity, this ancient circuitry keeps us alive. A rush of love, anger, fear, or a craving isn't random chaos; it's the body's primal Morse code, tapping out, "You're still here–keep moving." Palpitations in the chest or a knot in the stomach are cues from our biological past, reminding us that survival has always depended on emotion. Our limbic systems don't stop at measuring meaning; they measure aliveness.

Practice: When a strong emotion hits, don't fix it. Flirt with it instead. Ask, "What are you trying to show me?" Imagine the feeling as an uninvited guest at a dinner party–dramatic, overdressed, and a little loud. Invite the emotion to be seated. Pour a metaphorical drink. Listen with intention. What does it crave–safety, validation, control, or attention? Then usher it out before it rearranges your furniture or gives unsolicited life advice. If you can, name the feeling out loud, as naming disarms the emotion. "Ah, jealousy, you old joker," or, "Hello again, grief–still wearing black, I see." The act of acknowledgement transforms emotion from a tyrant into a teacher. Over time, what once ruled your life becomes like a quirky relative. Likable, spontaneous, yet no longer in control.

Daily Humor: Some people have spirit animals. Mine is my amygdala, decked out in anxiety couture, strutting like panic is a lifestyle brand. It might carry a fear-of-commitment purse or a jealousy scarf for flair. If this seat of emotion had an Instagram, it would post nothing but dramatic selfies, cryptic captions, and blurry photos from minor existential crises. Remember: Your limbic system is high fashion, dramatic, and a little extra. You're still the one holding the shopping bag. When drama hits, declare the runway closed, toss the scarf over your shoulder, and step off in style.

BONE #6 COLLARBONE OF CONNECTION

THE SPACE BETWEEN US

If the spine keeps you upright and the ribs give you structure, the collarbones are where life reaches out, literally and metaphorically. They are the subtle hinges that allow you to extend your arms, offer a hand, or give that perfectly imperfect, half-measured hug. Think of the collarbones as tiny, unassuming bridges that connect you to the world, balancing closeness without collapsing under the weight of another human's existential baggage.

Humor rides along with this connection–in the squeak of a hinge, the accidental bump of a shoulder, and the laughs that break the tension when you overreach or underperform. The collarbones are the hinge between self and other, between your messy, flawed humanity and the equally messy human you reach toward. Welcome to the Collarbone of Connection; where arms reach, boundaries bend, and humor always saves the day. Before we get too sentimental, let's admit: every deep connection begins with at least one awkward lean-in.

The Hinge Between Self and Other

Connection is not about losing ourselves; it's about hinging ourselves open so that something shared can enter. The collarbone sits right beneath the chest and arm, defining the space between holding close and reaching out. In relationships, friendships, or any encounter with "the other," we discover our own edges. Simone de Beauvoir's work explored this contradiction, showing how "the self" discovers "the other," not as something to own, but as an individual whose freedom is just as crucial as our own. On the modern end of existential thought, Emmy van Deurzen, an existential therapist and philosopher, reminds us that encountering others requires authenticity: we must show up, not as masks, but as flawed, contradictory selves.

Life is messy. You reach out, and the mirror of the "other" sometimes reflects your own shadows of insecurity, guilt, and unmet expectations. I've seen this play out in my life, whether trying to deepen a connection with family, friends, clients, or strangers. I speak my truth and get met with a mix of nods, silence, or discomfort. De Beauvoir would say that authenticity requires us to face this risk. Van Deurzen encourages us through the anxiety, suggesting that the "other" is not just someone else, but part of what defines our self. When we hinge toward others, we hinge toward something larger than individual meaning.

Sure, I find it hilarious how often that hinge squeaks. The awkwardness of saying, "I need help," the tiny betrayal of forgetting a birthday, or expecting someone to read your mind instead of telling them. Even ancient Stoics, including women like Hipparchia of Maroneia (often overlooked in history), emphasized the virtue of connection—showing strength and shared moral resolve are not just for the self but for the "other" in community. Modern voices like Elizabeth Brake, Pema Chodron, Martha Nussbaum, Brené Brown, and Maya Angelou push this further: connection is not weakness; it's tender, deliberate, and courageous.

Connection doesn't guarantee closeness. Sometimes the other pulls away; sometimes, we do. Yet, knowing the collarbone is there—that liminal space—allows you to act from a place that honors both your freedom and the other's. Opening the chest is about letting life in, even when life smells of spoiled milk and awkward encounters. The collarbone is a subtle hero, a fulcrum that demands structure and flexibility. Extending your arm is like saying, "I'm present, a little off-balance, and open to connection," even if it sometimes leads to minor collisions. Picture your collarbone as a tiny stage manager holding everything together while you flail, wave, or gesture dramatically—yet undeniably alive.

Next, we'll explore how to carry this connection steadily, opening with courage and bending under the human weight of vulnerability. Think of it as emotional weightlifting—you can't bench-press belonging on day one. The trick is to flex just enough openers to keep from snapping, and laugh when your internal hinge squeaks under pressure. Connection's warm-up routine would be awkward and shaky, like an early morning stretch, but weirdly satisfying.

Opening the Chest, Extending the Arms

Opening the chest is about letting life in, even when life reeks of rotten eggs and awkward encounters. The collarbone is a subtle hero, a fulcrum that demands both structure and flexibility. Extending your arm is your way of saying, "I'm here, flawed, unsteady, and ready to connect," even if you accidentally knock over a glass of red wine or misjudge the reach. Think of the collarbones as an existential jazz-hands moment–absurd, slightly theatrical, but human.

Vulnerability is a true workout for your existential collarbone. You can stiffen against it, fold inward, or open fully, risking a fraction of discomfort. There is comedy in overreaching, in brushing someone's shoulder when you meant a handshake, or in struggling to hold space for another human while juggling your own insecurities. Even Aristotle might raise an eyebrow at the balance required here, while Camus laughs at the absurdity. Rollo May would gesture knowingly, reminding us that courage is rarely a spotlight. Courage is the repeated act of reaching despite the unknown.

Practicing this reach primes us for the next act: noticing the weight we carry, and the hands we hold, and the shared loads of existence. Extending the arm isn't only symbolic; it's rehearsal for intention, humor, and the occasional blunder. After all, the collarbone is the pivot point that lets us reach for life without detaching entirely.

Brene Brown reminds us that "vulnerability sounds like truth and feels like courage," asserting that "truth and courage aren't always comfortable, but they're never weakness." In her work, vulnerability is not an admission of failure. Instead, it is the practice of keeping the heart ajar: daring to be seen when every instinct urges retreat. When shame contracts the body and silences the reach, vulnerability expands it, offering options where fear would prefer stillness. Brown reminds us that "vulnerability is the birthplace of love, belonging, joy, courage, empathy, and creativity." To extend the arm, then, is to take part in this paradox: to move toward others while trembling, to open the chest though the air is thick with uncertainty. Brown might call it the anatomy of connection; it's the invisible musculature of empathy, laughter, and belonging. Open that chest–just try not to let the draft mess up your hair.

The Hands We Hold

The weight we carry is not always visible, yet we feel the pressure on our shoulders like an overstuffed backpack filled with responsibility, regret, and randomness. Sometimes, the burden is heavy enough to make us stoop; other times, it's light enough to forget we're carrying anything at all. Until, of course, the AI (artificial intelligence) assistant reminds us of a missed meeting or a memory pops up on social media. Whether ancient Stoics, modern psychologists, or your neighbor who swears the Wi-Fi is conspiring against them, we all understand that existence comes with weight. The trick isn't shedding the weight completely; it's about learning which parts to share and which to bear alone.

Hands hold more that coffee mugs and cell phones. Our hands carry trust, support, awkward high-fives, and the ever-so-often slap of "why don't you text me back?" When we reach for another person, we discover our hands can literally and symbolically lift some of the load. Carl Rogers would nod here, observing that connection itself can be therapy, a mutual recognition of effort and vulnerability. Even Rollo May would point out that courage manifests in insignificant gestures:

the stretch of your arm, a steady grip, and the willingness to say, "Yes, I see you, and I'm here."

Our hands are more than tools; they open and close, reach and retreat, sometimes clumsily, and other times hold with the perfect measure of strength and tenderness. Modern thinkers might call this emotional intelligence, older philosophers call it virtue, and AI may call it data points for human cooperation. Despite everything, the situation is consistent: we eventually gain the skill to share burdens across connections in order to avoid being crushed by the profound absurdity of our circumstances. Even life's faux pas–a dropped phone, misread social media cue, or that text sent to the wrong person–become part of the existential orchestra. They imperceptibly remind us that the weight we carry is not solely ours, nor the hands we hold entirely theirs.

Finally, there's something unmistakably human in the shared weight we bear. We can laugh at life's absurdities, breathe through tensions, and still reach out again. There's humor in the misalignment of expectations and reality, grace in steadying someone else, even while you struggle to hold your balance, and awe in the micro-miracle of mutual support. The collarbone, the hinge between self and other, is not just a bone; it's a symbol of our capacity to extend, to hold, to carry, and above all, to keep connecting. In doing so, we prepare to enter the space where support becomes tangible and offering becomes conscious.

Arms Wide, Ego Tight

We like to think our support for others is a conscious choice, a chivalrous lifting of burdens. However, support often starts beneath the surface. Sigmund Freud famously described the human mind using the analogy of an iceberg. The vast majority of the mind, like the bulk of an iceberg, exists beneath the surface and is entirely unconscious. This inaccessible reservoir contains our deep-seated instincts, traumatic memories, desires, and basic drives. The unconscious mind exerts a powerful, unseen influence on our daily behavior and our feelings.

The mind's visible segment only portrays consciousness in this way. This is our awareness in any moment: our current thoughts, perceptions, and immediate feelings. The area just below the waterline is the preconscious. While it may not be a priority at the moment, we can access the information readily, just like we do with our memories and kept knowledge. Freud theorized that internal conflicts among these three levels, particularly the unconscious drives battling conscious reality and moral constraints, are the source of much psychological anguish. It's humbling to realize that what drives us isn't always what we think, especially when our unconscious keeps editing our life mid-sentence.

The Comedy of the Iceberg

Let's get creative. Picture an actual iceberg drifting in open water. Above the surface, the berg is dazzling, crisp, and photogenic: it mirrors our conscious intention to help each other. Below lies a hulking, jagged mass of forgotten grudges, childhood echoes, and the snacks you swore off but still buy. In theory, this is what Freud calls the unconscious; I call this the slow-motion comedy of self-sabotage. Instead of a lifeless body, the autopsy of existence diminishes this floating piece of the psyche through the friction of perception and wit. Admitting a clumsy motive or laughing at our own hypocrisy is like breaking the ice, allowing us a quick, chilly view of the deeper, darker currents below. We uncover the motives that compel us, gaining insight into not only what we hold on to, but why we hold on.

Shoulders of Support

Suddenly, the comedy of the collarbone comes back into play. The shoulders, the literal platform for life's book of burdens, are also the bridge for our arms: our reaching, our offering. When we carry solely from the unconscious, our support may appear or feel like martyrdom; when we carry with awareness, support becomes mutual, even playful. Shoulders of support, hands of offering are not a self-help mantra per se, but an anatomical reminder that the same muscles that hold weight can also extend a gift. In practicing this, we shift from performing heroics to taking part in a collective connection. Forget Atlas with the heavens; imagine two friends balancing a wobbly IKEA shelf, realizing, much like Freud's iceberg, that most of what's going on (missing scores, or failing to read instructions) lies beneath the surface. One friend holds the manual upside down, convinced the answers hide in secret code, while the other wrestles with a loose screw and existential despair. Somewhere between minor bruises and laughter at their own clumsiness, they discover the true meaning of teamwork: shared struggle, shared humor, and a vague promise never to trust pre-drilled holes again.

The Reach of Relationships

Reaching toward another person is not only a gesture of the arm. This reach is symbolic, a reversal for the life you want to build–a preview of the comedy show of being human with other humans. Every time you extend your hand, be it for a handshake, a hug, or an ill-formed side hug that morphs into a shoulder pat, you're testing the architecture of trust. As a pivotal structure, the collarbone allows for the balance of connection and independence, making every motion a discreet illustration of valor.

Contemporary thinkers such as Esther Perel teach us that intimacy is not a fixed, harmonious state, but a dynamic tension. Intimacy is the perpetual choreography between the self and the shared life. Perel's raw, honest humor hits on point: they should exchange the myth of "happily ever after" for the genuine work of "happily in progress." Every move toward a partner, friend, or foe is an act of balancing a fundamental yearning for autonomy. Often, we find ourselves poised at the edge of another personal world, attempting to read the signs—to knock, to wave, or cross a boundary. In this existential dance, the beauty lies in the attempt's grace.

Alignment Meets Embrace

On the whole, we shape our relationships through reaching toward others, not through grand declarations, but through small repeated acts. Checking in, listening, showing up when it's inconvenient, saying sorry when we err, breaking through vulnerability and shame by saying what we feel—all these make way for human connection. Every reach is a risk, and every risk we take reshapes our connection with others, as well as our sense of self.

In the underbelly of this reaching, an invisible anatomy is hard at work, far beyond the bones and muscles you've met. Hidden organs form life's vital connection as we trust our heart to pump, the liver to filter our curiosity, and our lungs to expand and contract with awe. Alignment meets embrace here in the comical halls, where your inner workings mirror your outer reach. As you slip into the next existential insert–the organs, and on to Bone #7–you discover that fearlessness is not a heroic pose, but a living circulation of courage moving through every part of your being in the world.

EXISTENTIAL INSERT: THE ORGANS

Vital, invisible, and delightfully ridiculous

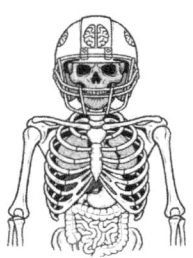

Beneath the bones, muscles, and the grand structure of your spine and collarbone lies an invisible control tower: the organs. These systems run the show, even if you don't notice. The heart isn't just a romantic prop. It's the pilot keeping everything airborne and calm after surviving countless near misses. Each beat manages the traffic of oxygen, nutrients, and emotional panic. The lungs act like a radar, expanding and contracting with every breath even as thoughts spiral around deadlines, regrets, and existential angst. The liver protects you from system crashes caused by curiosity, stress, or lost luggage, as it filters out the biochemical messes and metaphorical nonsense.

The kidneys, like seasoned deck officers, manage the delicate balance of fluids, electrolytes, and patience. They remind you that life isn't just about motion–it's equilibrium. The stomach, pancreas, and intestines function as logistic specialists, collaborating to ensure the delivery of energy to all parts of the body. Though flight plans change rapidly, these specialists ensure the mission continues. Even the spleen, often overlooked, coordinates defense protocols, proving that heroism doesn't always get applause, yet keeps you upright.

Practice: Imagine each organ sending a tiny radio transmission of gratitude to your conscious self. The steady beeping of your heart announces, "All systems go!" Your lungs whistle, "Runway clear!" Your liver signals, "Filter engaged!" Allow yourself to laugh at the absurdity of a command tower inside your own body, marveling at how these silent operators manage daily chaos better than any mission control you've ever seen. You should take a bow, or perhaps even give a salute to your own internal crew, because the show of your life would never get started, let alone take off, without them.

Daily Humor: Today my organs are running a flight with no pilot training. Mental cabin pressure is dropping. The engines are sputtering, and no one knows which way is up. Fingers crossed. I hope someone packed a parachute. Heck, maybe your spleen is judging you right now for even reading these words. Remember: even when the cockpit is on fire, your body somehow lands the plane.

BONE #7 FEMUR OF FEARLESSNESS

The bone that carries you through dread

An unsung hero of audacity, the femur carries us forward when hesitation tempts us to stay down, stay safe, or overthink the consequences of trying something new. From leading into a career change to attempting ballet moves you watched on YouTube, the femur reminds us that courage is less about perfection and more about motion. Without these bones, you'd be stuck in place–on the couch, literally. Welcome to the Femur of Fearlessness; strap in, stand tall, and prepare to wobble boldly into the adventure of being. Side effects may include spontaneous leaps, audacious decisions, and laughter so loud it echoes off your own thighbones.

The Unknown

The femur is the longest and strongest bone in the human body. To flex it, even symbolically, suggests building a core, foundational strength–the kind necessary for a successful existential leap. Stepping into the unknown is like standing at the edge of a cliff, staring down into a foggy horizon filled with both opportunity and existential terror. The philosopher Arthur Schopenhauer might grumble about life's inherent suffering, yet he would encourage the thrill of approaching fear head-on, realizing that it can bite you, even if only with a nibble. The humanistic psychologist Erich Fromm reminds us that freedom entails risk, and risk demands responsibility. Each movement into uncertainty carries the absurd burden of consequence. Amid the chaos, the poet Maya Angelou would undoubtedly offer the words "Still I rise," and in these words, courage would find a rhythm to guide it, even if fear has you momentarily paralyzed.

Existential horror slyly seeks purchase while we plan our leaps. Existentialist Kirk Schneider describes this terror brilliantly as the contraction and expansion of being–the feeling of free-fall where the world retreats and invites in search of balance. Contraction, or terror, is the impulse to pull back and cling to the precipice of the cliff, demanding the world be small, certain, and all-knowing. It's the moment fear forces your breath short and muscles tight. Expansion is the opportunity: the leap itself, where the self opens up to possibility. Here lives the thrilling realization that your choice is the only anchor you have, and the world is now as vast as your courage.

Pema Chodron steps into this tension with the simple advice to "lean into the sharp points," prompting us to meet the contraction of fear with tenderness, rather than aggression. She teaches that when we try to "fix" ourselves, we often make things worse, resulting in a more comical and complicated situation. This compassionate self-acceptance is the internal work that becomes the symbolic femur for the leap. In here words, "we can meet our match with a poodle or a raging guard dog, but the interesting question is: what happens next?" It's in that "next" moment that our humanity limps toward wisdom, armed only with tenderness and a decent sense of humor.

The realization that we must create meaning for ourselves, rather than having it readily available, is a dizzying, yet wonderful, experience. It's the dizzying realization of simultaneous resistance and surrender: the contraction of self, desperately clinging to the known, fighting the disorienting sense of groundlessness, followed by expansion: a gasp of release when fear transforms from a free-fall into balanced potential.

The unknown, for example, doesn't care whether you are prepared. The air may smell like burnt toast or desperation; stepping forward is the only way to find out what's on the other side. Humor here becomes a life raft, floating above the abysmal unknown, reminding us that even in terror, incongruity is always near. The first laugh in the void is the mind's victorious realization that our fear is itself a laughable performance. In this recognition, if we must create our own meaning, we may as well start with a laugh, finding the gravity not in the fall, but in our decision to leap.

On top of this, fearlessness is less a trait and more a practice of engagement. Every step into uncertainty flexes a metaphorical femur, strengthening your resolve even when the ground shifts beneath you. We tilt, we wobble, we flail, we misstep, and even face-plant in different circumstances. Yet, in every folly, there's information, insight, and laughter. This is where irony meets reality: we are alive, and alive amid awe and absurdity. The free-fall of life holds precious, teachable moments–a terrifying and instructive space, a gym geared for the mind, body, and spirit.

In truth, leaping into the unknown, or "taking a leap of faith," asks you to confront your inner self, not just the external world. This is where your inner landscape meets the chaos outside. Anxiety, desire, death, and curiosity swirl together, forming a storm that tests courage at every level. To move forward is to acknowledge that life's tension and beauty coexist in the same space. Each step becomes a negotiation in trusting the process, leaning into fear, and embracing uncertainty with open arms.

Even in treading through this darker exploration, there's room for the comic. You might trip, miscalculate, or forget your own name under pressure; yet, the act of taking a chance is an audacious defiance of stagnation. To walk into the unpredictability of life is to accept the absurdity of your own life, and in doing this, prepare yourself for another challenge. The symbolic femur of fearlessness carries you forward, the strongest bone reminding you that being courageous is structural, internal, and, most importantly, hilarious when viewed from the right angle.

The Courage to Be (Lost)

The theologian Paul Tillich, in his book The Courage to Be, described courage as: "the affirmation of one's being despite nonbeing." It sounds lofty until you realize he was talking about something deeply ordinary: the unspoken decision to get out of bed when life feels hollow, stagnant, overwhelming, or unrecognizable. True courage isn't about slaying dragons; it's about the heart's defiance, refusing to run from the grip of fear. To be lost, Tillich might say, is evidence that you are still searching–still awake enough to care where you end up.

Confusion, then, becomes a kind of compass. When what once held meaning falters, like when your GPS is on a loop of recalculating, the courage to be lost is the act of continuing into uncertainty, anyway. Tillich wrote in the ashes of war, where meaning itself burned out. Today, our anxiety looks different: an existential overload scrolling through news feeds, reels, algorithms that conflict with synchronicity, and curated lives that make us feel both connected and unseen. Still, the question remains the same: how do we keep affirming life when it refuses to make sense?

Maybe this is the answer: we keep moving, laughing, and connecting. One does not simply receive meaning from the "heavens." It's not something that is given to us. We shovel it together out of love, grief, awkward conversations, and half-baked dreams. Death looms, of course– the ultimate horizon, the blank space on every map. Tillich would argue, and perhaps rightly so, that courage is not the absence of despair, but the act of affirming life within spaces of existential angst. To be lost, then, is no failure. Being lost is the purest, most human form of faith, enrobed with the willing to wander in wonder while breathing light in the darkness.

Freedom Isn't Free (Neither is Lunch)

Freedom sounds noble in theory, like something you'd carve into a monument. Freedom is more like being handed the helm of the ship in the middle of a storm and told, "You got this!" Kirk Schneider calls this the "awe of existence," the groundlessness we feel when we realize no one is actually in charge. Rollo May and Louis Hoffman might add that our anxiety isn't a sign of weakness; it's admitting to being alive. In this sense, anxiety is proof that we are awake.

Irvin Yalom considers death as the "backdrop" against which freedom plays out. The simple knowledge that we will die one day is a clear sign that our time on this earth is not unlimited. Hence, we had better choose something–anything–before the curtain falls. Most of us, of course, respond by scrolling, snacking, napping, or in the state of procrastination. Existentialism understands this; life doesn't mock our avoidance, it nudges, "You can sleep later."

Ultimately, freedom isn't free; it costs your comfort, your excuses, and your ability to claim the external world for your own meaning. The universe gives no refunds; yet it offers moments of levity if you're paying attention. A little humor helps digest the heaviness; it's Fate's blue-plate special where incongruity is the main course and laughter is the tip you leave for surviving another day.

Trip, Fall, Learn, Repeat

Growth rarely announces itself with a drumroll; it shows up wearing scraped knees and the look of a deer in headlights, accompanied by a sigh. As one of the modern torchbearers of existential-humanistic psychology, Louis Hoffman brings to our attention that we don't find meaning in triumph, but in participation, such as being willing to show up, stay stable, and remain curious. The so-called failures we dread are often proof that we're still alive enough to make a choice, to risk something. Therefore, one should apply this brave fundamental principle and use it for traversing, rejoicing, or struggling through unfamiliar settings, not just consider it as an idea.

Anxiety is a light, not the enemy, but the vibration of freedom. Essentially, anxiety is a sign that something meaningful is at stake.

Similar to May and Tillich, Hoffman considered anxiety as the very essence of our existence, a clear sign we are conscious, alert, and able to make our own decisions. These teachings remind us that with every failure we experience, we are walking the edge between safety and expansion, between comfort and discovery. To fall is to feel, and to feel is to know you're still in the dance of life.

One can find humor even in death, which is the ultimate, final mishap in life. Ernest Becker, author of The Denial of Death, suggested that much of human striving is a grand, unconscious attempt to outwit mortality. Think about it: we build careers, write books, chase love, and post selfies, all hoping something of us will outlive the physical body. Laughter is perhaps our truest rebellion. Like the old saying goes, "What goes up, must come down." Every time we fall, we rise again; every time we find levity in the gravity of being, we defy extinction in our own unspoken way. Laughter becomes the rehearsal for transcendence, the small resurrection tucked between spilled coffee and cosmic awe. Collapse and creation, as Becker might agree, share the same staging, both testing being conscious.

That said, mastery is a rhythm, not the finish line. Trip, fall, learn, repeat. That's the existential waltz: awkward, honest, and entirely human. Life is not about perfecting the steps; we're learning to dance with our own fragility. The courage to keep moving after every fall is to find meaning in the missteps, and to turn falling into flight.

Strength in Motion

Fearlessness is kinetic; a series of deliberate movements through uncertainty, doubt, and delight. The femur of fearlessness doesn't just hold you upright; it acts as a lever, translating your inner courage into external action. Think of movement as becoming a rehearsal of being:

leaning into challenges, twisting when plans unravel, and stepping forward even when the Earth is quaking. Humanistic psychologists like Louis Hoffman might agree, noting that our capacity for movement–physically, psychologically, and relationally–is inseparable from our growth as autonomous beings. Here, strength is not about rigid perfection; it's the learned fluency of rising, adjusting, accepting, and persisting.

Beyond that, movement is a conversation between the mind and body, a dialogue that keeps the spine, the femur, and the rest of your bones engaged in this existential rehearsal. As David Mitchell wrote, "Our lives are not our own. From the womb to the tomb, we are bound to others, past and present, and by each crime and every kindness, we birth our future." Steps, lunges, and extensions carry the echoes of your choices, freedoms, and fears. Motion translates Kirk Schneider's concept of "contracting and expanding". As you stretch into the unknown, your body absorbs risk and fear, and then contracts to integrate the lesson; much like a dancer pausing mid-leap to collect balance before soaring again. Humor remains the lubricant of this motion. Finding humor in one's own shortcomings shows that fearlessness isn't about being perfect but a resilient and adaptable journey through the ridiculous aspects of life.

In summary, strength in motion invites you to be present, asking you to inhabit your body fully, trusting the biochemicals of courage encoded in your bones, muscles, organs, and nervous systems. As you flex your femur of fearlessness, you also strengthen your capacity for creativity, connection, and joy. Here, you become attuned not only to the burdens you bear, but to the rhythms of life surrounding you, moving with intention rather than reaction.

Now, it's time to shift focus downward, to the pelvic bone, the foundation of our physical and existential anatomy. This is where all life begins, all energy flows, and all connection takes root. The pelvis is the swivel between birth and death, creation and surrender, grounding us in the wondrous human dance. As we move from the femur to the pelvis, we find ourselves at the crossroads of regeneration and relationship; the space where stability meets the messy, hilarious work of being alive and kicking.

EXISTENTIAL INSERT: THE FAT

A Body's Best-kept secret

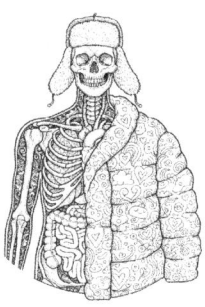

Etched into flesh, fat stands as a living testament to survival, comfort, and stubborn persistence. It cushions bones, shields organs, and regulates temperature to keep us alive. All of this, while the world is obsessed with size. Beyond biology, fat carries memory: the cement of feasts and famines, the traces of suffering, comfort, and survival. This living archive records every experience: sometimes praised, often criticized, but always wise.

Fat demands presence and rejects society's whims. Soft yet persistent, it mocks the idea that only the lean deserve attention. Treat fat as a testament to the truth that vulnerability and protection coexist. Softness doesn't equal weakness. Each layer is proof of endurance.

Practice: Place a hand on a body part you usually criticize. Feel its contours and textures, and the way it supports and protects. Instead of scolding, value how it insulates, gives warmth, guards organs, allows movement, and stores memory. Imagine each layer as a silent archivist, who keeps evidence of survival, choices, and resilience. Speak to it with gratitude. Laugh at its stubborn loyalty. Respect the labor it performs daily. This insulation is not a flaw; it's alive–a constant companion along the voyage through life.

Daily Humor: Fat ignores diets, Instagram, and societal expectations. It hoards organs, memories, and grudges with surgical precision. It protects you from the existential cold and demands credit as the unsung hero of endurance. All of your experiences rush back–a reminder that biology keeps receipts. Remember: fat never forgets, and neither should you.

BONE #8 PELVIS OF PERSPECTIVE

WHERE LIFE BEGINS AND ATTACHMENTS TANGLE

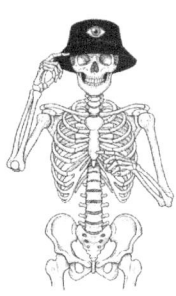

The pelvis is the foundation of movement, the cradle of birth, and the actor for both vulnerability and power. This bone allows us to explore themes of birth, death, regeneration, and relational humor. Here we can dig into the ways humans often over-rely on attachment, validation, and approval, while also laughing at our astrological and human tendencies, such as Scorpio death, Aries impulsivity, and the chaos in-between. Welcome to the Pelvis of Perspective; where gravity, absurdity, and very questionable life choices all have a front-row seat.

Center of Gravity

In the literal sense, the pelvis holds us upright, but more importantly, it anchors us in the theater of life. Imagine trying to balance while carrying the weight of your own expectations, other people's advice, and a vague sense of irony. That unsteadiness you feel? That's your center of gravity negotiating with your life choices, chuckling at your mistakes, and plotting revenge when you choose denial. Without this innate grounding, the strongest femur is just spinning in a universal current, disconnected from its center of gravity.

The apparent stillness should not trick you, because the center of gravity here is never truly stationary. It's a living, shifting compromise between fear, desire, and the occasional panic induced by remembering something you swore you'd never forget. Schopenhauer would likely call this area the bodily headquarters of desire and suffering, while Fromm might suggest the subtle negotiation between freedom and the need for approval. At this place, the pelvis, we feel the push and pull of life itself: gravity tugging, impulses surging, and the intermittent cosmic joke that grounds us in the cradle of humanity.

Humor is the lubricant of the pelvis, easing the friction not just of movement but of our human hubris. Comedy reminds us we are flawed beings, prone to mistakes, and endlessly improving. While the pelvis bears the weight of birth, death, and regeneration, this bone also carries our tendency to take ourselves too seriously. A well-timed laugh here humbles the ego, softens the insistence on control, and opens a space for curiosity, connection, and the occasional foolish dance move that proves we are alive, clumsily sublime, magnificent, and undeniably mortal.

At the core of the pelvis lies an unspoken intelligence, a quiet authority that steadies us when life tilts off balance. This is where gravity becomes personal, where we learn the art of holding ourselves without clinging. To find the center in this space is to recognize how easily we lean toward approval, attachment, and the comfort of being seen.

Genuine support–the pelvis reflects–starts within, not from others. By the invitation of the sacred bone, you understand and feel the contrast that exists between the concepts of grounding and grasping. The unwavering rhythm serves as a reminder that balance is not something that is forcefully attained, but achieved through a delicate process, a conversation that involves both letting go and holding on. The pelvis whispers, "We might move, to tilt, to lose form and then find it again." In this motion, we discover a deeper stability: one that doesn't seek validation, only radiance from self-trust, both rooted and free.

Boundaries and Bridges

If the pelvis is our axis of self-support, then relationships are the bridges we build outward from the center–often misshapen, sometimes under construction, and now and then, collapsing spectacularly in their stead. We are creatures designed for connection, yet modern life has turned intimacy into a paradoxical performance. Many reach for closeness through glass screens, swiping for soulmates while craving authenticity, and mistaking constant contact for genuine connection.

Seemingly, technology has made us hyper-connected and undernourished. We share more and reveal less. Even our latest conversational companion, AI, offers comfort without risk, presence without pleasure, and instantaneous feedback without the friction of being fully known. The experience is seductive because of the illusion of being safe. Virtual reality doesn't misread our time, forget our birthday, or need space. What appears to be perfection exposes our loneliness: the aching human need for something that can disappoint us, touch us, and still stay.

Attachment in the digital age has become a capsule of uncertainty. We're haunted by ghosting, distracted by endless options, and terrified of stillness long enough to allow someone to see us in our authenticity. Our traumas whisper that closeness is dangerous, while our mortality insists that being in a relationship is all that matters, even to one's detriment. We often oscillate between craving union and guarding autonomy, building boundaries like fortress walls, then yearning for someone to climb them to rescue us from the void.

Healthy boundaries aren't barriers or moats around the castles of our auras; they are bridges that know when to draw and when to drop. Boundaries mark the space where self-respect meets vulnerability: the space where we can say, "This is where I end and you begin," without losing the harmony of togetherness. In a way, the pelvis already knows this dance, yelling and resisting, opening and closing, and structuring movement and intimacy.

Perhaps the comedy of being human is that we're all trying to build a connection with tools we barely understand—half digital, half animal, forever improvising the architecture of love. Our attachments wobble, our defenses overcorrect, and still we try repeatedly. To stop reaching would mean to stop existing. Maybe this is the subtle brilliance of it all: in the unpredictable pursuit of connection, we come face-to-face with our own aliveness.

As Erich Fromm mused, love is an art we must practice; Esther Perel reminds us love is a dance between freedom and belonging; and

Irvin Yalom insists that facing our mortality sharpens our appetite for connection. Somewhere between those truths, in the soft hinge of the pelvis, we find both comedy and grace of desire itself, which brings us, inevitably, to the next step in our choreography–the dance of desire.

The Dance of Desire

Desire begins long before we know its name, humming along the roadmap of being human–in the pelvis's tilt, the quickening breath, and the electric pause between wanting and restraint. To be alive is to move between satisfaction and hunger, to live in the restless reality of reaching and retreating. Desire is the movement that shows we are ever-changing, unfinished, not whole, nor static. It's the body's way of saying, "Keep going, there's so much more to feel."

However, today's world has redesigned desire. Algorithms decide who we find attractive, dopamine spikes replace the slow burn of anticipation, and we've mistaken minimal friction connection for intimacy. Metaphorically, the dance floor has gone digital. We scroll through partners like playlists: skip, repeat, delete. Rarely do we pause long enough to hear the rhythm of another person's breathing. Our attention span has replaced our erogenous zone.

Yet, the body still refuses full editing. The pelvis, in its ancient wisdom, knows a different tempo. It understands that longing lives in tension, not resolution. The ache is not a flaw; this is the fuel that ignites the fire between souls. Desire, when honored, is not solely focused on pursuit–the aim is presence, even in knowing that everything we touch will someday vanish.

Trauma complicates this dance, teaching us that touch can burn, that closeness can betray, and that we earn safety slowly or not at all. Many of us learn to mastermind distance, disguising avoidance as independence. Yet, beneath all this composure lies an enduring desire: to be seen, mirrored, and moved. Desire asks us to risk being seen in our unguarded dance, to let someone trace the places we've armored, and maybe laugh when the music skips a beat. Humor is essential here, keeping the gravity of craving from becoming too heavy to hold. Anyone who's ever fallen in love, lust, infatuation, or something confusing in between, knows the absurdity of it all. The pelvis that anchors us can send us spinning out of control. Desire is a duo of dignity and pratfalls, elegance and entropy, ever reminding us that our biology is still funnier than our philosophies.

Authors like Esther Perel, David Schnarch, and Irvin Yalom have all explored the tension of the way intimacy thrives in mystery, not certainty; and how love deepens when we stop trying to force or master this personal attachment. As Camus may suggest, even the pursuit of desire is an act of rebellion against meaninglessness. So, we dance awkwardly, earnestly, sometimes in perfect rhythm, often with two left feet. We dance because the alternative—numbness and loneliness—is unbearable. The pelvis leads, the heart follows, and somewhere between love and laughter, we recall why we came here at all: to feel the music before it stops. There's a reason some have said, "Music is life." Love, it seems, is less a neatly folded map and more a GPS with a questionable sense of direction. You will take wrong turns, laugh at the detours, and sometimes end up exactly where you didn't plan to be.

Roots and Ripples

What happens after desire lands? After the pulse settles and the laughter fades, something quieter begins. The body, ever the archivist, keeps the record. Besides holding onto sensations of joy and suffering, our bodies also keep the fleeting memories of incomplete dialogues, including all the near misses, hypothetical scenarios, unrealized possibilities, and instances of things that should have happened. Encounters leave a trace, a ripple moving through muscles, memories, and meanings. The pelvis, once in motion, now steadies, listening to what still vibrates beneath the surface.

We have the freedom to move because no single place limits us, and we have no fixed roots. A look, a loss, a sudden kindness can deepen them as easily as it can uproot them. We like to imagine identity as stable, but the truth is closer to water: fluid, reflective, shaped by the vessels we pour ourselves into over the lifespan. Relationships are these vessels. Some homes treat us with tenderness; others crack under pressure. Despite the outcome, each of them teaches us something about how we give and receive nourishment.

Trauma also has roots–tangled and deep, warming our sense of belonging, and teaching the body to brace where it once opened, to contract where it once reached. As Bessel van der Kolk, author of The Body Keeps the Score, teaches us, the body doesn't forget what the mind tries to ignore. Yet, even these roots can soften with awareness. Healing is less about erasing the past than about re-inhabiting the present, letting new vibrations move through the old ones. The body, given patience and humor, can learn new ways of moving.

These vibrations extend beyond the personal. Every boundary we set, every connection we nurture, every joke we used to soften pain sends energy outward. Our moods, gestures, and silences shape the emotional climate of our relationships. Like stones dropped into water, we never know how far the circles spread. Maybe this makes living humbling and hilarious–our smallest motions can create tidal changes in someone else's sea.

Roots and ripples remind us we are energy, always moving. Our lives are molded and changed by the things we cherish, the things we have lost, and the choices we make to let go of certain things. To live consciously, we must notice the movement, feel where we tighten, where we flow, and where humility can still reach us. In that awareness, the pelvis becomes not just the body's center, but the witness to everything: the hinge connecting gravity and grace, between what grounds us, what moves through us, and the roots we become. Ultimately, it prepares us in subtle, inevitable ways to come full circle.

Full Circle

Coming full circle is not a conclusion; it's about noticing that our energy moves, traces, folds, loops, and resonates–a sway of the hips, a gentle shift in weight, the pauses between breaths that mark tension and release. The body's memory keeps a record of every movement and every experience, which influences how we understand both the world and our own selves. Steadfast yet mobile, the pelvis shows us that movement carries insight as much as expression, and that presence emerges not in stillness alone but in the dialogues between stability and flow. At its core, full circle is a delicate calling–showing us that endings often conceal beginnings. Our experiences, no matter how defeating, carry wisdom. Returning to center prepares us for what comes next: might it be laughter, failure, pleasure, pain, or reflection?

EXISTENTIAL INSERT: THE ARTERIES

Keep the beat, lose the drama

The arteries are the unsung heroes of our anatomy—silent and unseen, yet carrying life to every corner of the body. They move in purposeful silence, never pausing or questioning, sustaining the life force they carry. Arteries pulse, carrying blood like stories—weaving past injuries, joys, and forgotten laughter while delivering oxygen and energy to every dependent cell. Remarkable, isn't it? Something so tiny wield consequences so vast; if they could speak, perhaps they'd say: "Notice me. I am the muted workhorse of your existence."

These vessels are the ultimate teachers of kinetic flow and resistance. Life, like blood, must travel through bottlenecks, unexpected twists and the pressure of its own momentum. Arteries do not care about the route taken; they ensure we meet our destination of survival. They teach us that fearlessness is not about ignoring obstacles; it's about maintaining the pressure to push past the hiccups. Every beat commits to the rhythm of being, reminding us that existence depends on consistent delivery; though we often fret over goals, the arteries show that purpose lives in ongoing action.

Practice: Find your pulse–on your wrist, neck, ankle. Each beat whispers: "I am here." Let that sink in as your arteries chuckle: "You worry about deadlines, heartbreak, and overthinking. We've been working since before you could even spell 'air'." Let this pulse teach you that life unfolds in tiny, relentless moments, far beyond your conscious worries. Each beat resonates with the awareness that existence is miraculous, regardless of perception.

Daily Humor: Even blood shows up late sometimes, but it keeps the party alive. It rushes past your existential dread to deliver flammable oxygen, reminding you that your body has met every deadline since birth. Consider it your body's way of saying, "We've got this–try keeping up." Every beat is a relentless, judgmental reminder that the flow never stops. Remember: your vessels have been clowning around since birth, and the show must go on.

BONE #9 THE STAPES: SOUND MEETS SENSE

Small bone, big wisdom

Even the tiniest bones have big jobs. The stapes might be small, but it turns life's vibration into meaning–and chaos into comedy. Every creak, whisper, or unexpected sound teaches us that what we hear shapes how we move through the world. A quote that comes to mind is from Lisa Hayes: "Be careful how you talk to yourself because you are listening." Often, the smallest vibrations carry the loudest lessons. Welcome to the Stapes–where sound meets sense, and your eardrum gets the last laugh.

Just as the stapes translates vibrations into meaningful sound, our inner dialogue shapes our perception of the world. In the delicate interplay of life, even the tiniest signals–external sounds and internal thoughts–carry profound lessons that prepare us to eavesdrop on reality in all its subtlety. Sometimes, if you listen close enough, even your own hiccups can feel like the universe is trying to teach you something–or at least testing your reflexes. Those tiny spasms and twitches are proof that life vibrates beneath your awareness, that the body is always rehearsing its own symphony. Each involuntary movement carries a message: a pulse, a whisper, a reminder that consciousness doesn't conduct every note.

Eavesdropping on Reality

In case you didn't know or had forgotten, the stapes is the smallest bone in the human body, nestled deep in the middle ear. Shaped like a tiny horseshoe, nature's good-luck charm, it forms a delicate bridge between the eardrum and inner ear. Without this tiny bone, we wouldn't just miss whispers; we'd miss the music of life entirely. Consider this: a structure no larger than a grain of rice orchestrating symphonies, footsteps, laughter, and the slightest hum of existence. Even for those who are deaf, the lesson remains. Sound exists only as vibration; resonance lives in the body–in the pulse, the sway, the rumble beneath our feet–always reminding us that listening is a practice accessible to every human being.

Continuously, the world buzzes, vibrating at frequencies both noticed and ignored. Our senses, developed over millions of years for survival, are now bombarded with endless notifications, advertisements, and the low-grade static of other people's curated lifestyles. During this hubbub, the stapes shows that listening is not just hearing.

Tuning in is a conscious act of discernment. Life constantly whispers, but most of us listen to the wrong station.

To eavesdrop on reality is to notice the nuanced shifts in our bodies before the mind panics–the quick breath when someone nears your space, the tension held in the shoulder blades when we're stressed, the way our pulse beats when we glimpse at something of beauty. These signals are the language of existence itself: supple, precise, and from time to time, hilarious. Ignoring the language of being is like playing a drum solo in a library.

We often outsource our connection to life to two screens–watching flowing water on YouTube, scrolling curated sunsets on Instagram, meditating with apps–while the world moves around us, the breeze, the landscapes, mostly ignored. The stapes, in all its tiny glory, tells the story of life's three-dimensional vibe, not the two-dimensional one on the screen. Real listening requires presence, not pixels. To step outside, to feel your pulse align with the rustling of the tree's leaves meeting each other, or the rain misting on your skin, is a return to your body and the world all at once.

Modern life trains us to respond to alarms, not whispers. Fear and urgency have a louder frequency than curiosity and reflection. Profoundly, the stapes teaches us that even the tiniest structure can reveal truths our minds overlook and shape the way we experience the world. The smallest vibration offers what the intellect misses, whether we are moving forward in life or recoiling, whether our intuition is guiding us or we are merely reacting. This is a practice in humility, accepting that the body often knows what the mind pretends to understand.

Humor becomes essential here. Picture your stapes rolling its microscopic eyes as you scroll past another notification, miss the wind brushing your face, or argue with a stranger online. We are oblivious to the absurdity: the world broadcasts in surround sound while we wear earplugs. To notice the language of being–through the ears, skin of vibration–is to step off the treadmill of distraction, even if only for a moment, and realize we have been deaf to our own existence.

Succinctly, eavesdropping on reality is a homecoming. This act asks us to reconnect with the present, to tune into what is actually happening rather than the endless projections of fear, expectation, or comparison. The stapes prompts attention to what matters, inviting courage, curiosity, and humor along the way. When we hear what matters–whether through sound or resonance–we reclaim a world that is often too loud, too fast, and too hyper-focused on the insignificant.

Intuition vs. Fear

Intuition is the soul's unspoken instruction; fear is the mind's megaphone. Philosophers from Aristotle to Kierkegaard have hinted at this distinction: how are we sometimes called toward wisdom before our intellect catches up. Proverbs say, "Trust your gut," but in the modern world, we often rely on algorithms, likes, and constant validation instead of our own instincts. The challenge is distinguishing the slight nudge of instinct from the blaring panic of fear, a challenge requiring nerve and staying power.

At one time, our ancestors relied on fight-or-flight responses as life-saving tools. If a shadow shifted in the grass, a leap to safety was rational; if a predator prowled near the fire, fear kept the heart beating and the body alive. Today, shadows have become emails, notification pings, and social judgments. Fear, once a life-preserving signal, has now become something else. The irony is wicked: our primal mechanisms have survived evolution only to be co-opted by our smartphones.

External validation has become the new arbiter of "truth." Where once our bodies assessed risk and reward, now the mind checks notifications, likes, and comparisons to gauge safety. Intuition inquires, "Does this feel right?" Fear shouts, "What if everyone disapproves?" The result is a landscape littered with indecision, second-guessing, self-doubt, and missed opportunities. Our internal compass replaced by the compass of society leaves us strained between existential dread and digital distraction.

Learning to distinguish intuition from fear is a practice in presence. Sit with the tension in your chest, the flutter in your stomach, the hairs on your arms standing up. Ask yourself, "Is this sensation telling me to act, or warning me to protect?" Tending to your inner ecosystem calls for patience and stillness. The key is to giggle when your internal alarm clock is just your third espresso talking, or when your common sense is wearing a mask of crippling paranoia. We continue to persevere as our outside comedian finds joy in the absurd, even with our most critical notifications frequently being misdirected.

Without a doubt, intuition reconnects us to our embodied wisdom, to the very parts of ourselves that remember the rhythms of the world before social construction, culture and screens rewrote the rules.

Fear, when understood, becomes our teacher rather than a tyrant. Fear points us toward vulnerability, but not always to danger. The dance between intuition and fear is the human condition: learning to hear the whisper beneath the roar, to act on unspoken, transformative guidance, and to do so with humor, humility, and occasionally with grace.

Coming Home to yourself

Coming home to yourself is a less dramatic revelation than a hushed rebellion against a world that insists you are elsewhere. We have spent decades filling the void outside ourselves–swiping, scrolling, comparing, and binge-watching life through a screen, all the while the real ebb and flow of life's demands washed beyond our feet in the sand. The absurdity is in our face, hard to miss. Why watch flowing water on a device when the ocean hums for free, the wind tickles your skin gratis, and the trees are perfectly uncharted?

Phenomenologically, this encapsulates the art of knowing: the subtle sensations, the textures, the rhythms we skip in favor of notifications. Feeling your body, the rise and fall of your chest, the shifting of your weight as you walk, or the pulse under your fingertips is not a trivial detail. They are portals to a grounded, embodied consciousness. Nature and the body teach a simple truth: the revelation that presence is not a spectacle we scroll past, but a state of being we inhabit.

On a related note, the practice of coming home also demands rigorous honesty. Notice the ways we have outsourced comfort, entertainment, and self-validation. We chase external fixes because sitting with ourselves feels too big, too strange, or too quiet. When we pause, however, the outer world and the life inside resonate in ways we forgot were possible. A single breath, a step on dewy grass, and a place unfiltered by a screen are acts that reveal the radical presence found in the ordinary.

Once again, humor is essential in sensing the ridiculousness of your digital obsessions, where we attempt to connect with the world through pixels while ignoring the infinite textures of reality waiting just a glance or a step away. Laugh at yourself when technology gets humbled: when a hummingbird out-competes your meditation app, when an actual tree out-sways your yoga instructor, or when spontaneous music beats any playlist. The irony is spectacular: perceiving the contact between the digital and the real is the very path that leads us back to ourselves.

In the end, coming home to self is a practice of reclamation. It's learning that the self is not a destination to be reached online, but a landscape to inhabit fully. The currents of your own being, your senses, your body, and the world around you are seeking engagement, not curation. Arrival is the realization of three truths: you are enough, the world is at your fingertips, and presence means living wholly with the magnificent ridiculousness of being human. This is our most reliable form of home.

Resonance and Relationships

In the theatre of human connection, we are all actors learning lines that change daily. Today's dating scene presents a strange sight: a swipe culture where romance resembles fast food, people mistake dopamine rushes for genuine desire, and catfishing hides like an unwanted plot twist. Old-fashioned courtship, featuring patiently penned letters, lingering glances, and nuanced exchanges, is now often replaces disposable texts, "read receipts," and the lingering existential terror of "last seen."

Modern neuroscience explains why this feels so intense. Every notification ping is a little jolt of dopamine, an unseen sizzle of anticipation that can be mistaken for intimacy. Attachment styles (i.e., secure, anxious, avoiding) interact with these digital sparks, creating a feedback loop that can either ignite a meaningful relationship. Without it, we're left with hollow echoes of "likes," "hearts," or other tap backs; no one discerns the person behind the avatar.

Jay Shetty frames relationships as mirrors, not puzzles. The people we attract reflect the parts of ourselves we are yet to understand. When dating feels exhausting or foolish, it may be less about the wrong match, and more about the misalignment of your own internal resonance.

Communication remains the sturdy bridge of connection or, in existential comedic terms, the rickety rope swing between two lives. Talking to others is not about being articulate, but about creating presence and attentiveness. Active listening, honesty with an edge, and the ability to laugh at our own relational misfires transformed fleeting sparks into enduring fire.

We should notice the absurdities, such as the humor found in ghosting after a week of intense connection, the never-ending cycle of small talk that could fill a library, and the realization of being catfished multiple times in a month. Surely, there's existential beauty here, as the absurdity is our teacher. When we observe the absurd, we learn how to lean into resonance rather than resistance.

In their entirety, relationships–whether digital, fleeting, or lifelong–ask the same question of us: How do we show up? How do we remain present when our brains crave novelty? Or how do we love someone, including ourselves, without mistaking dopamine for destiny? In navigating these questions, we unveil that the comedy is not in failure, but in trying, again and again, with a wide open heart and mind.

Sidebar: The Absurdities of Modern Love

Swipe, sigh, repeat. Our thumbs have become philosophers: they ponder, they judge, they swipe left on existential dread. Meanwhile, the heart questions if only dopamine is speaking.

Ghosts of connections past. Ghosting used to be something in haunted houses. Now, it's your Saturday night date. Poof–gone, replaced by someone whose profile picture is a cat wearing sunglasses.

Catfish and other small horrors. There's a special circle in the dating underworld reserved for those who look like Charlize Theron but text like a robot.

Dopamine: the ultimate prankster. A notification ping feels like a cosmic wink, yet often it's just an algorithm playing Tetris with your emotional wiring.

Attachment style bingo. Welcome to the game of dating! Just pick secure, anxious, or avoidant, roll the dice and see if you can nail your type before the check arrives. Try not to let your existential panic ruin the vibe.

Courtship is dead; long live awkward texting. "LOL" and ellipses have replaced the art of lasting glances, and people think this somehow counts as meaningful conversation.

Communication as a rope swing. Hang on tight! Misunderstandings are inevitable. Humor is your harness. Vulnerability is your safety net. You will undoubtedly fall, but whether you laugh is up to you, though we highly recommend it.

Mirror, mirror, not on the wall. Your dating life is an elaborate setup designed to reveal all of your own unresolved baggage. The punchline is when the realization finally lands, usually deep into the texting marathon.

Existential takeaway. Love is messy, foolish, and occasionally glorious. Treat each misfire as a masterclass in patience, presence, and the art of laughing at yourself without guilt.

And so, after all the swipes, sights, and mini existential crises, something remarkable still happens. We meet someone whose presence cuts through the noise. The mind quotes, the body leans in, and the resonance between us becomes harmonious. The feeling of desire rushes forward–it doesn't announce itself with the immediacy of an app notification. Instead, it's a deep-seated pulse, felt within. This signal is so subtle that only the smallest elements of our being, akin to the stapes in the ear, can detect it. In doing so, they validate our capacity for astonishment. In a world of digital illusions, real chemistry feels rebellious. It's here in the space between certainty and surrender that the dance begins.

Anatomy of a Tempted Soul

Desire has terrible timing, often arriving when we least expect it–when we have sworn off love, are wearing our least flattering clothes, or are eating something profoundly unsexy. There it is: the unmistakable chime that isn't a text alert or notification, but a pulse from the body reminding us we are still, inconveniently alive.

Desire, at its core, is the physical expression of rhythm made flesh, especially when considering resonance as emotional frequency. Desire is how two nervous systems decide, consciously or not, to improvise. This is where the brain's neurotransmitters perform a clumsy ballet, with dopamine, oxytocin, and norepinephrine falling over themselves in a chemical frenzy of "what if." The result is a bizarre blend of chemistry and consciousness, laced with grace and chaos no algorithm could ever program.

We like to think of desire as a smooth, cinematic moment, but in reality, it's really awkward. Hands lose their purpose, the heartbeat transforms into a percussion section, and the inner philosopher suddenly forgets every line. We love so much of the desire in fantasy, where the lighting is perfect, the words are effortless, and we are, naturally, devastatingly composed. Yet, when reality cues the scene, it never unfolds as rehearsed. The kiss mistimes, someone laughs mid-breath, and what was supposed to be poetry dissolves into a clumsy force. Perhaps that's the truest pleasure of desire. Fantasy is flawless–but reality is alive. There's pure comedy in the loss of composure–a humble stripping away of the ego's monologue, letting instinct finally take the mic.

Psychologically, desire is paradoxical, connecting and dividing. Alain de Botton's work deconstructs the common romantic notion that love begins when we realize another person can fill the voids in our own existence. This love deepens only when we accept it cannot. Desire thrives in the space between longing and letting go.

Modern culture attempts to script and control desire with twelve-step seduction guides, flirtation formulas, and the endless scroll of advice columns. Yet, the genuine attraction has always been improvisation, involving equal parts uncertainty, timing, and play. Superficial actions do not build authentic closeness between people.

The true dance of desire, perhaps, is less about achieving perfection and more about maintaining presence. The core instruction isn't "come closer," but "stay real while you do." This means desiring without pretense, risking without guarantee, and laughing when the music cuts out. In this silent laughter, keep dancing anyway. At its core, desire is not about possession; it's about participation. Here, the universe shows us that being alive is moving toward something, even when we know it might unravel our essence. In this story that is coming apart, two imperfect individuals search for a connection, learning that genuine composure wasn't supposed to be attained within the moments of uncertainty, from the falls to the breaths of contentment.

Auditory Alchemy

Hearing the humor is the stapes' secret gift: the ability to translate the cacophony of life, love, and longing into a frequency that informs our steps. In fact, relationships themselves are absurd symphonies, where every note is a harmonious mismatch between expectation and reality. In the dating world, we imagine elegant courtships, candlelit exchanges, and poetic confessions; instead, we get voice notes that start with "hey" and end with ghosting. Humor is the stapes whispering, "Relax, you'll survive the missed cues and the catastrophic typos." Listening for the absurd, we hear not just what others are saying, but the rhythm of human weaknesses that makes connection simultaneously terrifying and exhilarating.

Desire itself is hilarious when examined through a lens. Neurochemically, dopamine and norepinephrine spark literal fireworks in our nervous system, while oxytocin and endorphins scramble to keep the situation socially tolerable. We seem hard-wired to misinterpret signals, stumbling through attraction with the grace of a newborn giraffe. Yet the inherent humor of all—including the wrong hand brushes, the fumbling words, the heart racing at inopportune moments—teaches us a vital truth of love. Far from perfect, love is a high-wire act with invisible netting, and laughter acts as the harness, letting us try again without falling to pieces.

Modern technology has made the absurdity of love even more visible. Dating apps, virtual reality meet-cutes, and AI chatbots create layers of potential delight and disaster together. We swipe, match, and stimulate intimacy with avatars programmed to be interesting, attentive, or impossibly perfect. Meanwhile, in the real world, subtle cues—a twitch, a stammer, a poorly timed laugh—all carry the authentic humor that no algorithm can replicate. The stapes, in its small, precise way, reminds us to tune in, to hear the jokes life writes between the lines of our nervous system, honoring the messiness of genuine connection.

Hearing the humor extends beyond desire and dating; it's the connective tissue of all relationships. We walk through life with everyone–friends, family, lovers, strangers–navigating a constant mix of miscommunication, jealousy, longing, tenderness, and loss. The nervous system actually encodes humor as a safety signal: laughter amid tension releases oxytocin, synchronizes our bodies, and reinforces our bonds. By attuning ourselves to the bizarreness and the unexpected punchline in every interaction, we refine resilience and strengthen the connection. Listening, truly listening, allows the stapes to function properly, translating life's chaos into rhythm, comedy, and heartfelt humanistic grace.

With laughter still resounding in our bones and the absurdity of desire all around us, we now turn from listening to reaching. If the stapes tuned us to the jokes of connectivity, the metacarpal is where the punchline meets action. Our hands, and by extension our choices, grasp at the meaning, trip over intention, and sometimes drop it entirely–only to catch it again in unexpected, human ways. Ahead, we'll explore bone number ten, which invites us to flex, hold, and create significance with the same playful abandon that keeps us flipping pages, swiping screens, and stumbling toward the tragic comedy of our own making.

EXISTENTIAL INSERT: THE NERVOUS SYSTEM

Where Neurons and Nuance Collide

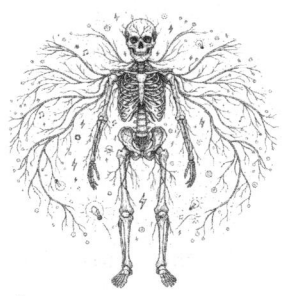

The nervous system has its own cast of characters: the central nervous system (i.e., brain and spinal cord) runs the show, while the peripheral nerves scatter mischief throughout the body. Even the autonomic system, with its sympathetic and parasympathetic branches, joins the fun, switching between fight-or-flight and rest-and-digest like a switchboard. Every blush, stammer, laugh, and pining entertains.

Neurons fire like little pranksters, while neurotransmitters toss sparks of dopamine and noradrenaline, and oxytocin strains to glue the chaos into something meaningful. Glances, awkward jokes, and a heartbeat out of sync are reminders: life is a rehearsal without a script, and the nervous system writes the punchlines. Yet, our nervous system knows better. It exaggerates, misfires, and reveals humor in minor misfortune, turning it into unforgettable moments. The fleeting sense of saying, "I love you," the sweaty palms on the first date, the laughs that burst out of nowhere–these are signature riffs. And the beauty? This chaos, this biological comedy, is not a flaw–it's a feature, teaching presence, attunement, and the audacity to keep trying despite the mishaps.

Practice: Forget taking five minutes to "meditate" on your nervous system. Instead, notice it misbehaving in glorious detail–fluttering stomach, twitching fingers, hearts skipping beats, and neurons firing like caffeinated imps. Smile, groan, or roll your eyes at each misfire. Pretend your sympathetic and parasympathetic branches are in a dual comedy: one flinging adrenaline, the other mumbling "chill-bro." Track one small interaction, like your phone dying mid-text, and watch your body improvise a punchline before your conscious mind notices. Every sneeze, blush, and laugh is a standing ovation from your internal cast of chaos.

Daily Humor: Your nervous system never follows instructions, yet somehow delivers absurdity on point. Trauma-based material, surprise adrenaline drops, and awkward silences–starring you every day. Palms sweat, stomachs flip, and neurons snicker at your life choices. Remember: your nervous system is the ultimate stand-up comic–and you, its unwitting audience.

BONE #10 METACARPAL OF MEANING

"Fingerprints are like personality—no two are the same." ~Sherry Punch

Before we dive in, it's worth meeting the metacarpals themselves. These five bones form the bridge between wrist and fingers, the scaffolding that allows us to reach, grasp, release, and create. Even though they are small compared to other bones, they have a monumental impact. Without them, the hand's gestures, the language of our actions, would become faint, weakened, or nonexistent.

However, the conversation of life does not exclude those who move through the world without hands. Anatomy does not define purpose, expression, and; the lessons of grasping, letting go, and shaping meaning translate across forms, whether through feet, voice, eyes, or intention. The metacarpals are our tactile metaphor, a way to explore the delicate balance between action, presence, and the subtle architecture of choice. This is our invitation to reach.

Hands-On with Life

Our hands are where consciousness meets the world. They are our first philosophers and our final confessors. Grasping preceded language: an infant's instinctive reach that says, "I'm here; I want; I belong." Long after words fail us, when speech retreats into the hush of old age or grief, the hands continue to speak. They clasp, they fold, tremble, and release. Through sign language, the hand becomes syntax itself: articulate, emotional, and precise. The concept brings to our attention that meaning transcends the boundaries of sound, finding its form through movement, expressed intention, and the power of silence. If the heart carries emotion, the hands translate it into motion; sometimes clumsy, sometimes elegant, always human.

Grief too, speaks through the hands. When someone we love is gone, our fingers still search for their shape in the dark, as though muscle memory refuses to accept absence. The poet Rainer Maria Rilke once wrote, "Everything terrible is something that needs our love." To reach toward what hurts is an act of defiance and devotion. The hands, stubborn in their reaching, perform this act again and again. We wash dishes, fold letters, touch the earth, hug each other. These are unspoken rituals of continuation. In mourning, touch becomes a philosophy: we can't hold the past, but we can touch what remains; and in doing so, we keep ourselves from disappearing with the loss.

In today's socially constructed world, we have become more adept at handling than holding. Our fingers fly across glass screens, scrolling through other people's lives, creating versions of our own. The tactile has given way to the visual, and we risk forgetting what it feels like to grasp someone who resists our touch. Philosopher Maurice Merleau-Ponty spoke of the "reversibility of touch." To touch is to be touched. The screen, for all its glow, offers no reciprocity. This artificial warmth, like a facade, did not stem from within, but was instead an external imposition. The live 'hands-in' now require an act of rebellion; one to make, to hold, to plant, to knead bread; to press a pulse and feel it answer back. These are the gestures that remind us we are still incarnate, still participants in the shared texture of being.

Purpose, then, is not something to be found, but something we shape. The hands give this away in the way we form clay, mend fabric, comfort a crying child, or bury the dead. Becoming is not lofty or abstract; it's a surreal, tactile process, grounded in the daily gestures of participation. Poet Mary Oliver quotes, "To pay attention, this is our endless and proper work." The hands are how we pay attention. They make attention visible. Even when empty, they carry the import of everything we've cared for and let go. There's a humble grace in this, the recognition that our meaning lives not in what we cling to, but what we dare to release.

Still, detachment is never easy. Grief loses its grip only to return in another form, disguised as nostalgia, yearning, or art. The Japanese practice of kintsugi, which is the art of mending broken pottery with gold, embodies such a truth. Although something shatters, it may not return to its original form but can still become more alluring. Our lives are like a kintsugi experience, and stories fill the cracks instead of gold. Every fracture, every moment of breaking, becomes a part of our construction. Elements that were once viewed as detrimental are now integrated into the design. The hands know this instinctively. They do not judge the work as imperfect; they continue shaping, smoothing, repairing. Meaning, like earthen clay, takes form only through contact, through what we touch, and what inevitably slips through our grasp.

Rarely do we discover purpose through a grand revelation. It emerges through repetition, and the insistence on doing. To hold, to let go, and to reach again are divine gestures of becoming. What we try to hold sculpts us, and what we cannot keep humbles us. This is a humbling process, sometimes maddening, and the closest thing we have to transcendence. To live hands-on is to engage fully, even when what we touch changes us beyond recognition.

Perhaps this is the meaning of becoming: not to master the art of holding on, but to accept the art of release. Our hands teach us that letting go is not a failure of strength, but a signature of trust that leaves room for what's coming. Throughout our lifetime, with the hands still learning their own lessons, we turn from the intimate wisdom of touch to the ways our choices, actions, and grasp of life shape meaning itself. Sometimes life gives you a firm handshake; sometimes it leaves you dangling in midair. Either way, don't forget to wave and enjoy the ride.

Hands and the Space Between

The space between hands and time is more than distance; it is liminal. For example, liminal space is the threshold where connection becomes possible, where meaning is co-created, and where we learn the practice of patience and presence. Too close, and the intimacy smothers; too far, and the moment slips through our fingers. The boundary is constantly being tested; every gesture, and every accidental knock serve as a rehearsal for establishing liminal space. Even when alone, we prepare for this interaction, trying to find meaning though we are uncertain, as we rehearse a conversation that might never receive an answer.

Think of rings, scars, and fingerprints as markers of the tiny territories of meaning. These marks tell stories; they are the traces we leave behind. Our hands, acting as storytellers, create invisible lines in the air that shape and define the liminal space that exists between the shelves. Evidently, we will never solve the problem of distance, but the effort remains a teachable lesson in everything. In trying, we learn the act of holding on and letting go, of touching lightly and deeply, and how we meet each other halfway, be it physically or imaginatively.

Crucially, the space between us is not a void; it's full of memory, anticipation, and the slapstick comedy of our need to matter. Throughout our lifetimes, as the hands continue their lessons, we move from the intimate wisdom of touch to the broader arrangement of action, choice, and consequence. Knowing what to do rarely makes doing easier. Purpose is rarely neat; it often arrives disguised as error. The clumsy work of self-discovery starts with these ridiculous, half-hearted gestures. Sometimes, the best we can do is fumble forward, trusting the next step will reveal itself–eventually, maybe with a bit of laughter.

Fumbling Toward Purpose (Becoming)

Becoming isn't a straight line, but more like trying to text with stiff fingers. You think you're typing out a message of clarity, but what appears is gibberish, auto-corrected by circumstance. Somehow, the person who received the message can "read between the lines," or at the very least maintain the fiction of comprehension. Our lives are a series of such clumsy transmissions, half-meant gestures that trace the outline of who we're becoming.

The act of becoming demands humility you can't fake. We like to imagine growth as effortless, like a final garnish placed on the main course of life. In reality, growth is closer to being raw ingredients: peeled, bruised, subjected to intense heat, and left to marinate in uncertainty over time before true flavor emerges. Maybe that's the point: meaning doesn't just arise from perfect presentations but from endurance. The Japanese concept of wabi-sabi finds beauty in imperfection; perhaps the human version is existenti-silly. The key is laughing at the random bumps and bruises of existence, then confidently insisting they are part of the original design.

Becoming is less about the emerging 'self' and more about the relentless process of losing ourselves repeatedly. Every time we think we've found our purpose, life hands us a plot twist: a heartbreak, a profound loss, or a new beginning disguised as failure. The trick is not to read these detours as mistakes, but as textural additions; the essential details of our character. Even before the impact, the sound of a dropped object announces its outcome. Maybe we weren't supposed to hold on to purpose as if it were something we could own. Purpose is fluid, responsive, always slipping just when we think we have a grip. Remember to look at life's follies with grace, and have the courage to keep reaching–not because we know what comes next, but because the moment itself is what keeps us alive.

EXISTENTIAL INSERT: THE SKIN

Where the world begins and you end

Skin is both shield and mirror, a living interface between inside and outside, self and world. It registers warmth, cold, pleasure, and pain, translating the chaos of existence into sensation. Every line, mark, bruise, or scar is a testament to our lived experience. It remembers the laughter that left shivers, the tears that traced invisible paths, and the countless touches that shaped our sense of being. Skin is intimate and exposed, tender and resilient–the body's armor that protects with boundaries while insisting on connection. In fact, skin is the largest organ we carry, bearing witness to who we are and how we move through the world.

Practice: Skip gentle mindfulness—your skin is running its own reality show. Run your hands over it anywhere you like and notice the chaos: scars plotting revenge, freckles conspiring with wrinkles, stretch marks judging your life choices. Every bump, line, or mole is a character in the drama of you. Pinch, poke, tickle—see how it reacts. Feel the flirtation in shudders, the teasing in a ripple, the secret sigh when warmth hits you just right. Your skin is a diva and a workhorse, enduring sunburns, scrapes, and poor fashion decisions without complaint. Giggle at it, and marvel that this oversized, opinionated organ keeps you intact while running a covert commentary on your life, often throwing a sarcastic tantrum with an unexpected chill.

Daily Humor: Your skin knows all your secrets and still has not leaked them…yet. Judging from the occasional breakouts, it has opinions. Absorbing misapplied sunscreen, scratches, and stress, it's a passive-aggressive friend that stages dramatic rebellions at the worst possible time. The best part? It's the most honest organ you own. It never sends a vague text; it flushes crimson when you bluff and ages right on time—a way of saying, "Your warranty is non-negotiable." Remember: It will haunt you with flaws and rogue chills for years to come.

BONE #11 METATARSALS OF RETURN

WALKING THROUGH LIFE ONE FOOTPRINT AT A TIME

This book began at the top, a tour of the mind's architecture and the body's scaffolding, moving from the Skull's authority down to the Pelvis's grounding power. Yet all that wisdom, all that wit, all that fearlessness, must eventually find its place in the world. It's through the feet that our entire existential structure (our balance, our humor, our anxieties, and our audacity) meets the actual, messy earth. The feet, our silent anchors, carry all our intentions, turning our thoughts into miles. As we complete this anatomical audit, we turn to the most fundamental structures–the ones that have literally been beneath us all along–ensuring the journey, however absurd, continues.

Heel Yeah, Let's Go

Our feet are the unsung comedians of our anatomy, tripping, slipping, and showing us that gravity always has the last laugh. They bear the weight of our existential angst, from stubbed toes to the residual footprints that map the chaos and comedy of our lives. Although the previous chapter praised the hands for their ability to create and play, the feet carry us through it all–step after humbling, inevitable step. Every footprint is both literal and metaphorical, a scroll displaying the places we wandered, the paths we braved, and the extended, looping journey back to ourselves.

In fact, the feet are most humble yet most stubborn. Together, they forge the terrains of time and act as balancing coaches–essentially, the travel agents of our soul. Stark reminders that movement is not optional–be it a hike through Nietzsche's mountainous thoughts, pacing in late-night reflection, or shuffling to the refrigerator for the third time in a philosophical meltdown–the feet are our lifelong coach. Every step we take is a dialogue with gravity, with the earth, and with the subtle little chatter inside that sighs, "Will I ever arrive?"

The answer is yes, though not to some faraway destination. We arrive at ourselves. We return home with sore arches, blistered heels, and footprints fading behind us, because every outward path is also an inward one. Even people who cannot walk, who lack feet, or whose steps are still, still move through imagination, memory, and adaptation. Because the journey's spirit endures, it shows that people's physical forms do not limit their resolve to move forward.

The Soles of Being

Our feet are more than mechanical instruments for standing, stepping on LEGO blocks, or slipping on banana peels. They are both esoteric and rational–the philosophers of motion. Consider how all your weight, and every celebration, and every failure converge upon these small foundations. The soles are the first point of contact with the Earth, feeling every encounter–from a cool brush of grass to the metaphysical bumps in the road. The feet experience life without us thinking about their selfless actions. They are our primary somatic sensors, translating paths into awakenings and discomfort into awareness.

Each footprint leaves behind a story, an existential poem. Experiences that occur early in life, like taking first steps, dancing for the first time, or setting out on journeys away from home, frequently evoke a mixture of hesitation and uncertainty. Yet within those wobbles live the bold strides of becoming. Footprints are proof that we have lived–each step a record of our participation in the ballet of living.

Walking is a meditation most people ignore. When we pace, stroll, or wander, we are not just burning calories; we are in the rehearsal of life. Every step is a mantra, a conversation with the past, and a movement toward your future self. Our footsteps resound Nietzsche's eternal return–marking the space where we keep moving and keep learning until our outer self mirrors our inner one.

The feet also teach us humor in humility. We stub toes, slip, trip, wobble, and ache–yet they carry us, anyway. In imbalance we find grace; in clumsiness, we remember that being human is not a smooth or elegant trot. Reflexology and other practices show us that feet hold more than bones and muscles—they hold energy, nerve endings, and ancient maps of the body's inner world.

Finally, the soles are our grounding shamans. Each step is a note in the music where weight meets gravity and desire. They teach us patience, attentiveness, and endurance. Reflecting on our footprints—where we've been, how far we've traveled, and how far we still might go—gives us a glimpse of returning to self.

Reflexology and Hidden Maps

Somewhere between mysticism and the massage therapies lies the curious gospel of reflexology. This metaphysical map proposes that every inch of the foot corresponds to an inner landscape—press one point and the liver quivers, touch another and forgiveness suddenly feels possible. Whether it's pseudoscience or poetry, the feet were telling stories long before we could stand upright to listen.

Think of the soles as roads that never reach GPS, where landscapes of tension, rolling hills of pressure, and rivers of connective tissue near the heel. Each step redraws the map, and every unspoken emotion leaves its own topography. Reflexology reminds us that the world exists both underfoot and within. The ache beneath the arch may be the grief you swallowed last year; the tightness in your toes, ambition trying to outrun time.

Modern life has dulled our feet into submission. We pad them, bind them, elevate them, and then complain when numbness sets in—as if they should thank us for the imprisonment. We forget the feet were once sagas of survival: barefoot messengers, market dwellers, pilgrims who prayed by walking. To reconnect with them is to remember that wisdom isn't always cerebral; sometimes it's cracked, calloused, and solely in need of a divine soak.

Essentially, reflexology becomes less about pressing points and more about listening. Beneath the surface radiates an entire nervous mythology—conversations between the body's geography and memories. If the brain keeps the archives, the feet keep the gossip. Unlike the mind, the feet—like the hips according to Shakira—do not lie. They creak, twitch, and pulse with the truth of where you've been and what burdens you still carry.

So go ahead, take off your shoes, find the tender spots, and press gently. Don't worry about healing your spleen or achieving energetic equilibrium. Ask, "What is this place trying to tell me?" You might discover that the map to wholeness was literary under your feet the entire time.

Feet Have No Plan

The feet, bless them, have never cared for blueprints, five-year plans, or a spiritual GPS. They wake up each day with the same modest ambition: to carry you somewhere—anywhere—preferably without face-planting. While the mind drafts grand stories of fate and the heart auctions for meaning, the feet show up—wordless, unpretentious, and already halfway down the hall before anyone has agreed on the destination.

We often speak of finding our way through life as though life comes with a clear set of directions. The feet know better. Life is mostly a series of wrong turns that somehow still lead us home—to ourselves. Should there be any unexpected detours, they will be completely forgiven without exception. In truth, uncertainty is their element. Movement is their language.

Perhaps this is the secret: the brain fears the unknown, but the feet thrive in the mysterious. Built to wander, to test and miscalculate steps, they find grace in falling. Given the current circumstances, it's important to realize that the feet represent phenomenological humanistic comedians, humorously struggling with the absurdity of existence, and poking fun at our preoccupation with maintaining control. Each step lands a punchline to the question of being, proof that experience comes first and understanding, if it comes at all, always limps behind.

Feet don't need a plan; they are the plan. So when feel lost, take comfort in this small anatomical truth: even the parts of you that carry the most weight do not know where they're going–somehow, you always arrive.

Footnotes of the Self

If the feet could leave footnotes, they would annotate every misstep, pause, and detour with sly commentary–the unedited record of how you actually lived. Every step is a stamp of experience in the ground: where you hesitated, charged ahead, or sidestepped the complexity of life. The soles archive even the tiniest actions and movements that might have gone unnoticed. Calluses mark persistence, arches hint at resilience, and bruises or scars show impressions left in the sands of time.

Over time, the feet become autobiographical, writing the stories of what we carried, where we've been, what we ran from, and the possibilities of where we are going. The feet hold no grudges, only evidence of the distances endured, balance regained, and our biopsychosocial survival. When the last page turns, the feet will have written more of your story than your hand ever could.

With this thought in mind, look down. Those are not just your feet. They are the punctuation marks that keep you from floating off the page and lasting proof you have lived. These unsolicited footnotes tell your messy, hilarious, and esoteric story, step-by-step. They've seen every direction you swore was "the right way" and politely declined to comment. Feet, after all, are the philosophers of the body—grounded, patient, and amused that your head thinks it's in charge.

EXISTENTIAL INSERT: THE SOUL

The only organ that doesn't need a pulse

The soul is an organ without anatomy, a compass without a needle, a comedian without a microphone, yet somehow, it runs the show better than any part of the body. It doesn't require oxygen, blood flow, or a pulse to leave an impression. Your soul exists in the margins–in glances, hesitation, and laughter–all of which influence the body, the mind, and the chaos we call reality.

Unlike muscles or bones that obey gravity, the soul obeys the strange: curiosity, pining, or absolute foolishness. The soul has a flair for timing, dropping insights at the oddest moments—usually when you're brushing your teeth or walking to the fridge. It's both invisible and indispensable, a reminder that life is gift-wrapped in seriousness and ridiculousness. This tendency for the strange means the soul loves irony, thriving on contradictions—asking you to surrender while insisting you take up space; to fail while learning a lesson; to exist in a body that's busy checking the time, the temperature, and the expiration date on the milk.

Practice: Pretend your soul has a personality—and make it highly opinionated. Place a hand over your chest and notice the chaos it stirs: mischievous thoughts, absurd impulses, sudden insights with poor timing. Ask yourself: "What does my soul want me to witness?" Don't wait for a calm answer—it will respond with random ideas, ridiculous images, or gut reactions that bend reality like quantum entanglement. Snark at it, roll your eyes, or tsk at its timing. Watch how it prods your body to twitch, your mind to dart, and your plan to detour, all while insisting it's the star of the show. The soul doesn't RSVP, but it shows up anyway—sometimes with drama, sometimes infuriating, always unforgettable.

Daily Humor: The soul is like that friend who ghosts the group chat but somehow always shows up—late, dramatic, and armed with the exact sarcasm you needed. It's the ultimate lurker, seeing everything without ever commenting. Remember: your soul has a backstage pass to all your existential moments, and it's laughing through the absurd.

BONE #12 HUMERUS OR HUMOROUS

THE LAST BONE YOU'LL EVER TAKE SERIOUSLY

Welcome to the final skeletal entry: the humerus, skeletal jester of the body–a bone that refuses to take itself seriously, yet somehow holds up the arms that gesture, embrace, and point at the absurdities of life. Fun fact: the humerus is the longest bone in the upper arm and connects the shoulder to the elbow–a literal bridge between power and play.

Unlike the soul, which wanders invisibly, or the metatarsals that march us toward self-discovery, the humerus thrives in motion, misalignment, and the occasional pratfall. This bone reminds us that even in structure there's comedy, that every lift, swing, or shrug carries the potential for enlightenment and laughter.

The humerus asks a humble question: why not? Why not laugh at your own mistakes, at gravity, at the awkward complexity of life itself? This serves as a reminder that absurdity is inherently part of who we are, that humor is a vital capacity just like the muscles we exercise, and that even the lightness we experience, including physically, is a means of persevering. Here we examine the final intersection of anatomy and philosophy, where the practical meets the ridiculous, and the undeniable joy of being human tempers the serious business of existing.

The Bone That Laughs at Gravity

The humerus does not simply exist to lift, swing, to throw; it exists to remind us that gravity is relentless and funny. Physicist Richard Feynman once described the universe as "not only stranger than we imagine, it's stranger than we can imagine." Our humerus embodies that strangeness: a bone engineered for leverage, yet perpetually subject to the comic timing of tripping over your feet, spilling glasses of wine, or flailing during an unexpected high-five. Even Stephen Hawking may nod in approval: here is a bone that literally supports our attempt to defy—or at least bargain with—the laws of physics. In the grand experiment of life, the humerus is nothing if not our lever and our lab assistant, ensuring that for every elegant throw, there's an equally comedic collision with reality. This awareness of bodily absurdity primes us for the next act, where courage and motion intertwine in the dance of existence.

From a philosophical perspective, the humerus is a small, tangible mirror of human absurdity. Dostoevsky might argue that the human condition itself is a series of misfortunes, small and large, and the humerus is the literal instrument of many of these mishaps. Each time we swing, lift, or make any gesture, it functions as a mark of existential punctuation, highlighting both our successes and shortcomings as we exist in the world. Given his penchant for cosmic perspectives, Neil deGrasse Tyson would likely chuckle at the irony of our stargazing potential being linked to everyday mishaps like stubbing toes and bumping elbows.

The humerus is more that comedy; it's also a symbol of resilience. Consider the architecture of this bone: strong enough to support weight, flexible enough to sway, and always recovering from strain. Like humor itself, the humerus is an existential metaphor you can touch. Much like the unavoidable nature of life's complexities, the effects of gravity also represent something that we cannot escape. Humor reaches its potential in the same way the humerus works with other bones, muscles, and joints, when people share it, put it together, and maybe make it a bit disjointed. This is the perfect introduction to the joint ventures that make life and laughter possible. Every shared flop, spilled coffee, or missed step reminds us that chaos is best enjoyed as a duet. Together, we discover that even mistakes have choreography, and that life's absurdities come with applause we didn't know we were earning.

Joint Ventures in Life's Irony

Life rarely unfolds in perfect isolation, and neither does humor. Like the humerus requiring the shoulder, elbow, and forearm for any movement, our experiences of irony, mischief, and comedy are often born collectively. Our funniest moments, from the spilled milk to the panic over a frozen phone screen, show that we fail best when we fail together. Henri Bergson once observed that comedy arises where the mechanical meets the living, and in this instance, the unexpected absurdity provides life's mechanics around us.

Even Richard Dawkins, the evolutionary biologist, might agree. In his work, The Selfish Gene, he explores how behaviors that foster cooperation and communication can be evolutionarily helpful. Shared laughter, accidental failures, and ironic coincidences are not just amusing: they are vital social signals that strengthen trust and adaptability. Humor, like these key traits, is co-created and thrives in partnership. Whether we are helping someone who just fell or laughing at a mutual mistake, these moments show that life's irony is a co-authored experience, not a solo performance.

Dostoevsky argues that suffering is central to the human condition, but our shared ironic moments provide a crucial counterbalance: relief, connection, and meaning. Life's ironies are not about fate mocking us; they are about participation, with every slip and correction contributing to the collective dance between the inevitable and unexpected. Humor thrives because it's relational, reflecting the beautifully messy coordination of our bodies, minds, and circumstances. Sometimes the universe sets up a crime scene just to see if we notice the evidence—and maybe take notes. Every minor calamity becomes a case study in human absurdity, just as every elbow jab, accidental humorous bump, or nervous giggle becomes the forensic psychologist of your own life.

Today, take time to notice your own interactions. Watch as these tiny misalignments collide and become something to laugh about. In and through each interaction, you enter a joint venture with life itself, discovering that irony isn't a punishment, but your companion along the way.

Laughter As Leverage

Humor is not a byproduct of survival; it's a tool, a fulcrum, leverage we use against the absurdities and burdens of existence. The humerus acts as a lever for physical work. Similarly, laughter provides emotional leverage, letting us momentarily lift the weight of life with surprisingly little effort. Nietzsche once suggested that we should say "yes" to existence, despite its suffering and repetition, and perhaps we often punctuate that "yes" with laughter. Humor is our existential crowbar, prying open perspective and loosening the grip of angst.

Consider the social dynamic of laughter: it's contagious, binding, and sometimes irreverent. A well-timed joke or shared laugh can transform a tense encounter into an opening for connection. Evolutionary theorists like Dawkins would note that this is no accident; laughter functions as a signal of safety, alliance, and adaptability. When we use humor in social situations, we are not only diffusing tension but also reinforcing the invisible scaffolding that holds human communities together–one snort, one chuckle, or awkward giggle at a time.

Even on a personal level, humor functions as leverage against the internal weight of life. Viktor Frankl, the logo-therapist and Holocaust survivor, observed that even in the most extreme circumstances, a person could find "the space between stimulus and response," in which choice (often humor) lives. A witty comment, a playful self-observation, or even laughing at life's mask of irony can shift our perception. Laughter, in this sense, is a psychological lever, lifting the mind when the body or circumstances might feel immobilized.

Conversely, leverage alone does not guarantee a clean lift; sometimes we must allow ourselves to fall, only to rise differently. The beauty of humor is that it teaches us how to fall without breaking, how to pivot when expectations collapse, and how to catch ourselves in the delightful gravity of life's missteps. Each miscalculation becomes a stepping stone, a lesson in improvisation and perspective. Laughter isn't just a tool; it's a practice in buoyancy, preparing us for the next swing, the next unexpected ascent—what I like to call the art of falling up. Everyone tries it, whether they realize it, and the punchline is always coming.

The Art of Falling Up

Falling isn't failure. It's an experiment, a lesson in momentum, and a rehearsal in improvisation. The art of rising, "of falling up," is recognizing that each tumble offers an opportunity to recalibrate perspective, find humor in the slip, and re-engage with the world differently. In a sense, the humerus has been practicing this all along: it bends, rotates, and swings continually to convert misalignments into smooth, effective motion.

Philosopher Simone Weil spoke of gravity not just as a force, but as a metaphor for limitation and attention. In falling, we encounter our own limits, our habitual seriousness, the weight of expectations, and also, the potential for delight and insight. Similarly, artist Marcel Duchamp challenged the very notion of "correct" orientation in space with his readymades; he reminded us that perspective is fluid and that what appears to be a fall in one frame may be a flight in another. Falling up, then, is not literal but metaphorical: it's learning to adjust swiftly, minimizing the damage from a fall, and to see the upside of what appears downward. Even in motion, there's improvisation. Dancers and athletes understand missteps become teachable moments, that gravity is a partner in play rather than an enemy. Life, humor, and human connection follow similar principles. The art of falling up invites us to accept our misfortunes, notice the laughter hidden in mishaps, and to use them as leverage for creativity, insight, and even joy.

Constructively, remember that falling is neither shameful nor to be feared; it's a natural, necessary, and often hilarious aspect of movement, humor, and living. The lesson is simple: the next time you stumble–psychically, socially, or existentially–observe, adjust, and lift yourself by your bootstraps of curiosity. Falling up is a dance, a lever, a wink from the universe showing that misfortunes carry wisdom, with a side of laughter.

The Subtle Comedy of Being

As the humerus shows, movement conveys purpose, even if that purpose is flawed. Beyond grand gestures and clumsy swings lies unspoken humor: the irony of simply existing. The subtle comedy of being lives not in failure, but in micro-moments that reveal life's inherent absurdity. It's in the involuntary shrug of a shoulder, a yawn that sweeps contagiously across a room, and the beautiful imperfections of our everyday blunders.

In biology, proprioception mirrors this: it's the body's innate awareness of itself in space. Without even thinking, the humerus collaborates with ligaments, muscles, and nerves to maintain balance, adjust posture, and accommodate the unexpected. This automatic orchestration is constantly punctuated by happy accidents: a laughable wobble, an awkward tilt, or a spontaneous gesture that feels perfectly staged. The body's comedy is its continual improvisation, confirming that the beautiful mess we call life is simultaneously precise and wonderfully chaotic.

Albert Camus described existence as "the absurd," not in the sense of ridiculousness alone, but as a tension between a human desire for meaning and the universe's indifference. The subtle comedy of being lives in this tension. Despite all seriousness, the body and humor keep their own timing. The humerus joins the jest, lifting and swinging for the unexpected, teaching patience, grace, and the self-aware smirk.

Subtlety is the deepest form of leverage. Unlike a dramatic fall or a loud joke demanding attention, the small ironies, the barely noticeable misalignments, the minor shifts, and the soft laughter at oneself profoundly shape our awareness. Observing them is to witness the comedy of being in its purest form: an intimate, universal dance of imperfection requiring no applause.

The Humorous Heart

If the funny bone keeps us from taking life too seriously, then the humorous heart keeps us from taking ourselves too seriously. The quiet organ of irony beating beneath our rib cages, pumping perspective through every chamber. Where the mind can spiral and the ego can inflate, humor steps in like a soft defibrillator, demonstrating that even the most dramatic pulse is still one beat among billions.

We laugh, not because life is easy, but because it is not. Humor is the psychological jester that walks into our mental courtroom and whispers, "Relax, you're guilty of being human." It grants us the courage to hold paradox: to love people who drive us mad, to grieve what we cannot change, to forgive what logic says we shouldn't. Each laugh dilates the emotional arteries just enough to let compassion circulate again.

A humorous heart doesn't deny pain; it metabolizes this burden. In the same way muscle grows through micro-tears, our sense of humor expands through life's ruptures. The heartbreak, the awkwardness, the absurdity of striving–all of this becomes compost for meaning when turned with a bit of levity. Somewhere between tragedy and timing lies the art of resilience.

Maybe this is the ultimate punchline of being alive: the incredible ability to laugh deeply while still caring intensely. The humorous heart marches to its own strange beat, for it can find the giggle in our chaos, embrace our contradictions, and somehow keep the entire body of our experience dancing to its unpredictable rhythm.

As this chapter closes, take a moment to feel your own pulse. Beneath every worry, every wound, there's a rhythm that hasn't given up yet. That's your cue, the set-up before the epilogue. Life's joke isn't cruel; it's unpredictable, messy, and sometimes absurd.

LIFE'S A PUNCHLINE: EPILOGUE

THE FINAL WINK

My last name has given me an appreciation for a good "punchline," whether it's a clever remark or a joke delivered at the right moment. Puns are more than just a peculiar characteristic; they're practically a genetic glitch I've learned to celebrate. Pun intended. Some might call me the queen of puns, and they wouldn't be entirely wrong. After all, how often does your last name set the stage for both comedy and self-reflection?

Life, as I have discovered, is nothing if not a series of setups and deliveries. From my debut performance at a funeral parlor–chest rising and falling in what I thought was my grandmother's final breath–to my years in the Navy; from classrooms to kitchens, my existence has been a long, winding, absurdist joke. The punchline? That all of this–the grief, the discipline, the mishaps, the late-night kitchen experiments–has been preparing me to recognize the humor embedded in the human condition.

This book is, in a sense, my autopsy of experience, laid bare with stitches of laughter. Each chapter, each "bone" of experience taught me to question everything; the Rib of Regret reminded me that mistakes are funny only if you survive them; the Funny Bone of Folly proved that self-deprecation is an underrated superpower; and finally, the Humorous Heart, where laughter, insight, and resilience converge.

The true punchline is not the bones themselves, but the way life gives you the timing, the chaos, and the chance to laugh, anyway. Life's ironies are not something to fear, nor are they a burden to bear. These absurdities are an invitation to notice the unexpected and to fall up through uncertainty. So, here we are at the end of the beginning of your walk in life with a new perspective–even a new perception. Having finished all the preparations and with the stage set, you can finally begin your performance, which everyone is eager to see. Everything is in place, including the jokes, the shadows, and the illumination. The spotlight warms, and the audience waits. In the middle of everything, the one who sees the timing, laughs at the chaos, and carries both struggle and joy–that's you, the reader.

Congratulations! You made it to the end; what more could any existential comedian ask for? Laugh, learn, survive, and take your existential mic drop.

BODY OF EVIDENCE

Endnotes

Angelou, M. (1978). Still, I rise. New York, NY: Random House

Aristotle. (2009) Nicomachean ethics (T. Irwin, Teans.). Indianapolis, IN: Hackett Publishing Company.(Original work published ca. 340BC).

Becker, E. (1973). The denial of death. New York, NY: Free Press.

Bergson, H. (1911). Laughter: An Essay on the Meaning of the Comic (C. Brereton & F. Rothwell, Trans). London: Macmillan.

(Original French edition Le Rite. Essai sur la signification du comique, 1900).

Brake, E. (2012). Minimizing marriage: Marriage, morality, and the law. Oxford, England: Oxford University Press.

Brown, B. (2010). The gifts of imprecation: Let go of who you think you're supposed to be and embrace who you are. Center City, MN: Hazelden Publishing.

Brown, B. (2012). Daring greatly: How the courage to be vulnerable transforms the way we live, love, parent, and lead. New York, NY: Gotham Books.

Chodron, P. (2002). When things fall apart: Heart advice for difficult times. Shambhala. (Original work published 1997).

Dawkins, R. (1976). The selfish gene. Oxford University Press.

de Beauvoir, S. (1948). The ethics of ambiguity (B. Frechtman, Trans.). Citadel Press. (Original work published 1947)

de Beauvoir, S. (1949). The second sex. (H.M. Parshley, Trans.). Vintage International. (Original work published 1949)

de Botton, A. (1993). Essays in love. London, England: Hamish Hamilton.

de Botton, A. (2016). The course of love. London, England: Penguin Books

Dostoevsky, F. (1992). Notes from the underground (R. Paver & L. Volohonsky, Trans.). Vintage International. (Original work published 1864).

Duchamp, M. (1973). The writings of Marcel Duchamp (M. Sanouillet & E. Peterson, Eds. & Trans.). De Capo Press.

Einstein, A. (1955, May 2). Old man's advice to youth: "Never lose a holy curiosity." Life Magazine.

Epictetus. (2008). The Handbook (R. Dobbin, Trans.). Hackett Publishing. (Original work ca. 108 CE)

Epicurus. (1994). The essential Epicurus: Letters, Principal Doctrines, and Vatican sayings (B. Inwood & L. P. Gerson, Trans.). Hackett Publishing. (Original work published ca. 341-270 BCE)

Estes, C.P. (1992). Women who run with the wolves: Myths and stories of wild women archetype. Ballantine Books.

Feynman, R.P., Leighton, R.B., & Sands, M. (2011). The Feynman lectures of physics (Vol. I). Basic Books. (Original work published 1964).

Frankl, V.E. (2006). Man's search for meaning (B. Zweig, Trans.). Beacon Press. (Original work published 1946)

Freud, S. (2010). The interpretation of dreams (A. A. Brill, Trans.). Basic Books. (Original work published 1900).

Fromm, E. (1941). Escape from freedom. Farrar & Rinehart.

Fromm, E. (1956). The art of loving. Harper & Row.

Fromm, E. (1992). The art of being. Continuum.

Google. (2025) Gemini (Version 2.5). [Large language model]. http://gemini.google.com

Hawking, S. W. (1988). A brief history in time: From the Big Bang to black holes. Bantam Books.

Hayes, L.M. (n.d.). Be careful how you talk to yourself because you are listening. Retrieved from https://www.lisamhayes.com

Heidegger, M. (1962). Being and time (J. Macquarrie & E. Robinson, Trans.). Harper & Row. (Original work published 1927)

Hoffman, L. (2018). Existential guilt. In R. Woolfolk & S.A. Joseph (Eds.), The APA handbook of humanistic and existential psychology (Vol. 1, pp. 435-451). American Psychological Association.

Horace (23 BCE). Odes 1.11. In G.P. Goold (Trans.), The Odes of Horace (Loeb Classical Library). Harvard University Press.

Hubbard, E. (1900, December). Do not take life too seriously. The Philistine. Roycroft Press.

Jung, C. G. (1938). Psychological aspects of the persona. In Collected works of C. G. Jung, Vol. 7: Two essays on analytical psychology (R. F. C. Hull, Trans., pp. 154-172). Princeton University Press.

Jung, C. G. (1959). The archetypes and the collective unconscious. In The collected works of C. G. Jung, Vol. 9, Part 1 (R. F. C. Hull, Trans.). Princeton University Press.

Jung, C.G. (1963). Psychological commentary on "The Tibetan Book of the Dead." Princeton University Press.

Kierkegaard, S. (1987). Either/Or (H.V. Hong & E.H. Hong, Trans.), Princeton University Press. (Original work published 1843)

Kierkegaard, S. (1980). The sickness unto death (H.V. Hong & E.H. Hong, Trans.). Princeton Press. (Original work published 1849)

Kierkegaard, S. (1989). The concept of irony with continual reference to Socrates (H.V. Hong & E.H. Hong, Trans.). Princeton University Press. (Original work published in 1841)

Kierkegaard, S. (1985). Fear and trembling (A. Hannay, Trans.). Penguin Books. (Original work published in 1843)

Lee, B. (1971). The Way of the Intercepting Fist [Television series episode]. In Longstreet. Universal Television.

May, R. (1953). Man's search for himself. W.W. Norton & Company.

May, R. (1967). Love and will. W. W. Norton & Company.

May, R. (1975). The courage to create. W. W. Norton & Company.

May, R. (1981). Freedom and destiny. W. W. Norton & Company.

May, R. (1983). The discovery of being. W. W. Norton & Company.

Merleau-Ponty, M. (1962). Phenomenology of perception (C. Smith, Trans.). Routledge & Kegan Paul. (Original work 1945).

Mitchell, D. (2004). Cloud Atlas. New York, NY: Random House.

Navia, L.E. (1996). Classical cynicism: A clinical study. Greenwood Press.

Nietzsche, F. (1969). The gay science (W. Kaufmann, Trans.). Vintage International. (Original work published 1882)

Nietzsche, F. (1974). This spoke Zarathustra (W. Kaufmann, Trans.). Viking Press. (Original work published 1883-1885).

Nietzsche, F. (1968). Beyond good and evil. (W. Kaufmann, Trans.). Vintage International. (Original work published 1886).

Nussbaum, M.C. (1994). The therapy of desire: Theory in practice in Hellenistic ethics. Princeton University Press.

Oliver, M. (2003). Yes! No! In Owls and other fantasies:Poems and essays (p. 27). Beacon Press.

OpenAI. ChatGPT (GPT-5) [Large language model].https://chat.openai.com/

Perel, E. (2017). The state of affairs: Rethinking infidelity. Harper.

Plato. (1997). Complete works I(J.M. Cooper, Ed.). Hackett Publishing.

Plato. (2008). Symposium (C.D.C. Reeve, Trans.). Hackett Publishing. (Original work ca. 385-370 BCE)

Rilke, R.M. (1929). Letters to a young poet (M.D. Herter Norton, Trans.). W. W. Norton & Company. (Original work published 1929)

Rogers, C.R. (1961). On becoming a person: A therapist's view of psychotherapy.Houghton Mifflin.

Sartre, J.-P. (1964). Nausea. (L. Alexander, Trans.). New Directions (Original work published 1938)

Sartre, J.-P. (1992). Being and nothingness. An essay on phenomenological ontology. (H. E. Barnes, Trans.). Washington Square Press. (Original work published 1943)

Schnarch, D. (2009). Intimacy & desire: Awaken the passion in your relationship. Beaufort Books.

Schneider, K.J. (2009) Awakening to awe: Personal stories of profound transformation. Jason Aronson.

Schneider, K.J. (2017). The renewal of the hero: A psychology of self, courage, and awakening. Routledge.

Shakira. (2006). Hips don't lie [Recorded by Shakira & Wyclef Jean]. On Oral fixation, vol. 2. Epic Records.

Jay Shetty (2023). 8 rules of love: How to find it, keep it, and let it go. Simon & Schuster.

Schopenhauer, A. (1969). The world as will and representation (E.F.J. Payne, Trans.). Dover Publications. (Original work published 1818)

Tillich, P. (1952). The courage to be. Yale University Press.

Tyson, N.D. (2007). Death by a black hole: And other cosmic quandaries. W. W. Norton & Company.

Van Deurzen, E. (2009). Everyday mysteries: A handbook of existential psychotherapy (2nd edition.). Routledge.

van der Kolk, B.A. (2014). The body keeps the score: Brain, mind, and body in the healing of trauma. Viking.

Weil, S. (1952). Gravity an grace (E. Craufurd, Trans.). Routledge & Kegan Paul. (Orignial work published 1947).

Wilde, O. (1895). The complete works of Oscar Wilde. London: Methuen.

Yalom, I.D. (1980). Existential psychotherapy. Basic Books.

Yalom, I.D. (2008). Staring at the sun: Overcoming the terror of death. Jossey-Bass.

Yalom, I.D. (2017). The gift of therapy: An open letter to a new generation of therapist and their patients (Revised ed.). Harper Perennial.

Wittgenstein, L.(1953). Philosophical investigations (G.E.M. Anscombe, Trans.). Blackwell.

FINGERPRINTS

Touched by the Author

A chef, educator, and business owner, Dr. Punch develops the *Existential Pantry*—a space dedicated to existential coaching, culinary practice, and the psychology of wholeness. Through her writing, she brings humor and depth to questions of identity, purpose, and the art of living well. In a rapidly changing digital age shaped by AI, she invites readers to laugh at life's absurdities while discovering meaning, connection, and the occasional perfectly cooked meal—proving that a pinch of humor makes everything taste better.

As you close this book, may you leave something behind—if not answers, then at least a good laugh, a fuller plate, and fingerprints of kindness on the lives you touch.

Bone appétit.

Made in the USA
Coppell, TX
22 February 2026

72059588R00085